the 5 Minute Gardener

In Honor of
Margaret Riddle's
30 Years of Service

2008

the 5 Minute Gardener

How to plan, create, and sustain a low-maintenance garden

Brenda Little

Silverleaf Press

Silverleaf Press Books are available exclusively
through Independent Publishers Group.

For details write or telephone
Independent Publishers Group, 814 North Franklin St.
Chicago, IL 60610, (312) 337-0747

Silverleaf Press
8160 South Highland Drive
Sandy, Utah 84093

ISBN-10: 1-933317-79-5
ISBN-13: 978-1933317-79-3

Contents

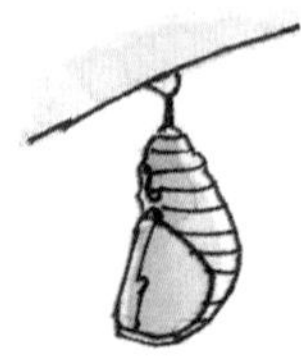

"There can be no other occupation like gardening in which, if you were to creep up behind someone at their work, you would find them smiling."

~Mirabel Osler

Introduction

Many people never attempt to grow a vegetable or flower garden because they believe they are too busy. "A garden takes lots of time and trouble—I'll wait until I've retired and have all day to spend in the garden," they tell me. Why wait? You need those flowers and vegetables now—especially if you have a growing family to enjoy healthy homegrown food.

For example, in recent years busy people have begun to shy away from planting flowers, which they see as time consuming, opting instead for so-called low-maintenance gardens which rely on a lawn surrounded by fast-growing shrubs, such as cypress, which are intended to provide greenery and privacy.

Gardens like this are boring and they still require regular maintenance. Lawns need frequent mowing and care or they become infested with weeds and, in hot dry weather will brown if not watered regularly. Shrubs selected for speedy growth soon need frequent pruning to keep them under control.

This is the dull side of gardening and it soon becomes drudgery when robbed of the enjoyment of seeing a garden full of flowers and, of course, one of the great pleasures of gardening—picking blooms for a vase or to give to visitors.

If you are missing the joy of flowers in your garden, the good news is that you can have a flower—or vegetable—garden without having to face up to hours of work.

If you don't have a lot of space to work with, don't worry. A well-organized container garden can produce good vegetables and some fruits. The small volume of soil will warm up faster in spring than the soil in the open garden. This gives a longer growing season.

You can also tend a good crop of herbs, which are easy to grow in pots and don't demand a lot of attention. In fact, excepting mint and basil, herbs will enjoy the drying out that's hard to avoid in terra-cotta pots. And you can get creative using a mixture of different styles of pots to create a pleasing group.

There are many options for the five-minute gardener. And remember, you don't need to spend all day working to have a successful garden. Just five minutes a day is all you need to keep flowers and vegetables watered, fed, healthy, and growing well.

Of course, you can't expect to be able to start a garden from scratch in five minutes. You will need to devote a weekend or two to planning and making the basic garden beds—ordering and perhaps collecting the essential additives such as compost and manure, seaweed, spoiled alfalfa hay or straw, and in some cases, removing weeds from the neglected garden patch you plan to use.

Careful and thorough preparation is important—it's the secret of success for the five-minute gardener. It involves some hard work, but it is enjoyable, creative, and good exercise too.

Once you have done the basic preparation of forming new garden beds or rejuvenating existing ones, you can maintain a flower and vegetable-filled garden by devoting just five minutes a day to its care. This book tells you how.

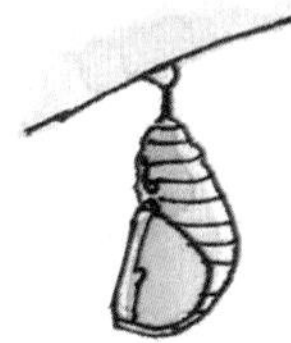

"Gardening is about enjoying the smell of things growing in the soil, getting dirty without feeling guilty, and generally taking the time to soak up a little peace and serenity."

~Lindley Karstens

chapter 1

Five Minutes a Day in the Garden

The secret to success for the truly five-minute gardener is organization. Each of those five minutes has to be well spent in tending flowers or vegetables, not hunting for missing tools and something to fix the aphids. So the first step is to set up a five-minute gardening basket. This basket should be easy to find, but out of the way of curious children. It should contain: a ready-to-use spray can of insecticide; a spray can of all-purpose fungicide; snail bait; pruning shears; gardening gloves and strips of old nylon stocking for plant ties.

On your five-minute sorties into the garden, check for sign of pest invasion. Warnings include discolored, chewed, and curled foliage. Squash snails underfoot, or drop them into a bucket of salted water. Squash caterpillars if you can find them, spray with Bacillus thuringiensis (Dipel) or dust with Derris, if all you find is evidence of their presence. Rub off aphids or spray if there are too many to deal with individually.

Look too for signs of disease, such as powdery

mildew or other fungal diseases and either remove the diseased leaves and put them in the bin (never add disease to your compost bin) or spray. If a plant is in serious shape, toss it. The five-minute gardener doesn't have time to indulge in intensive care treatments.

Snip off dead flower heads with your pruning shears to encourage further flowering and treat yourself to a bunch to bring inside every few days.

Check soil for dampness at root level and water if soil is dry. Keep mulch over soil to prevent drying out.

Maintain a feeding program through the growing stages to encourage quick and showy results.

Steal a few more minutes from your day to linger in your garden enjoying its sensual delights.

Buying a Spade

When buying a new spade, test it at the store for weight, handle comfort, and length so that you can be sure of having something that suits your size and strength.

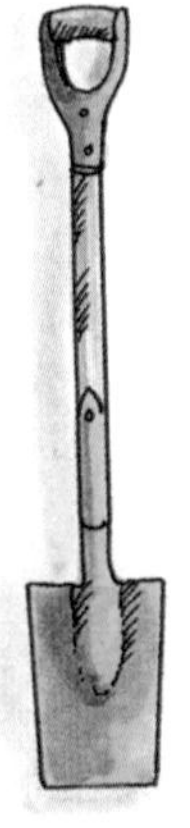

Using Tools to Tend the Garden

The five-minute gardener will not need a huge range of tools to tend the garden, but using suitable tools—sharp and clean and with good smooth handles—will enable you to work quickly and easily. Good sharp pruning shears are a must for any gardener. (If you are left-handed, buy a left-handed pair.)

Keep tools stored somewhere handy—on a wall in the garage or garden shed—so that you don't waste your five minutes searching for the right implement.

You will also need to have a few sprays handy

in case of insect or disease attack. The five-minute gardener will not have much time to spare to mix and measure, so rely on a safe, ready-to-use mixture in a pressure pack (pressure packs use safe propellants these days) or hand-pump container. Basic sprays include an insecticide, a fungicide, and a packet of snail pellets.

Whenever possible, use an environmentally friendly insecticide such as pyrethrum, soap (homemade or commercial sprays such as Safer), or Derris Dust.

The Five-Minute Tool Rack

Dutch hoe, steel rake, spade, fork, hand trowel

The Five-Minute Gardening Kit

Keep your basic requirements together in a basket ready to be carried with you on your daily trips to the garden. Suggestions for the basket include: a ready-to-use spray can of insecticide, a spray can of all-purpose fungicide, secateurs, gardening gloves, and strips of old nylon stocking for plant ties. The basket should be kept on a handy but high shelf, out of reach of children and pets.

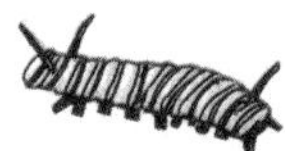

"It is like the seed put in the soil—the more one sows, the greater the harvest."

~Orison Swett Marden (1850-1924)

chapter 2

Soil Preparation

Being a successful five-minute gardener means spending a lot more than five minutes preparing your garden. Every hour you spend before planting means more time saved, as well as improved productivity once you have planted. By improving the soil to optimum health with organic matter, getting rid of weeds, and using a mulch to prevent their comeback, generating an ongoing supply of compost and installing a watering system, you really can be a five-minute gardener. It might take a month of weekends to get everything ready, so start now.

Don't attempt more than half an hour of heavy digging on your first day in the garden or your muscles will demand their revenge when you try to get out of bed the next morning.

Preparing the Soil

Be prepared to spend some time working your soil into top condition before you plant. This will give you great results later, when it really counts. First, dig over the beds with a hoe, removing any perennial weeds, such as onion weed, as you go. If the soil is heavy clay, treat it with gypsum, then water and fork it over two or three times a week until it becomes more friable. Soil that has some clay content without being too heavy can be treated with lime. Sprinkle 1½ tablespoons of lime per square foot (1 cup per square meter) over the soil and then lightly water and fork it in.

Next add liberal amounts of humus, such as compost, spent mushroom compost, rotted manure, strawy stable manure, or peat moss. Choose whatever is readily available. The addition of humus is important in sandy as well as heavy

soils, as it helps moisture retention. Add enough humus to raise the level of the beds by 2–3 inches (6–8cm). Dig it thoroughly through the top 4–5 inches (10–12cm) of soil. The humus will encourage earthworm activity and further enrich your soil.

Water the bed and leave it for a week to allow weed seeds to germinate. They can be lightly scuffed over with a steel rake or Dutch hoe. Any grass or perennial weeds that come up, such as oxalis, should be removed by hand and thrown in the bin. Annual weeds without seeds can be left lying on the bed to rot down as extra humus.

Making Compost

Every gardener, even a five-minute gardener, should have a compost heap or bin. Build a heap on the ground, or invest in a manufactured bin. There are many of these to choose from, including the compost tumbler, which speeds up the compost process. As long as you remember to turn the handle a few times every day, you can expect compost in about 10 days.

A mulching machine is a great asset if you have lots of prunings and leaves that can be shredded, though they are expensive and are probably best shared with gardening neighbors.

The mulch from a mulching machine can be

The Right Soil

Your ultimate aim is a dark brown soil the consistency of coarse bread crumbs that holds together well when you squeeze it in your hand. It might take you a couple of seasons to achieve this. Don't despair—keep adding organic matter.

Manure and Weeds

Manure from horse stables will often contain seeds from the horse feed, such as sunflowers and oats. These are easily controlled and can be composted. Milled cow manure purchased from a nursery should be weed-free, but paddock manure may contain undesirable weeds. If you are uncertain about the source of your manure, leave it in a heap for a couple of weeks and water it so that any weed seeds will germinate—and can be pulled out—before you spread it. This will ensure that you don't inflict something dreadful like nut grass on yourself. No five-minute gardener can afford the time to cope with an infestation of nut grass.

used directly on your garden bed or can be put into the compost bin or tumbler.

If you have plenty of space, make a three compartment set of bins using timber slats or, even more simply, chicken wire wound around stakes. One compartment is for current use, one is closed while it finishes the composting process, and the third is ready to spread. Into the bin go lawn clippings, vegetable and fruit peels, egg shells, tea leaves and coffee grounds, nut shells, contents of the vacuum cleaner bag, spent plants, twiggy prunings, fallen leaves, seaweed, and weeds without seeds or perennial roots.

To every layer of compost material, add a spadeful or two of soil or manure. Speed up the

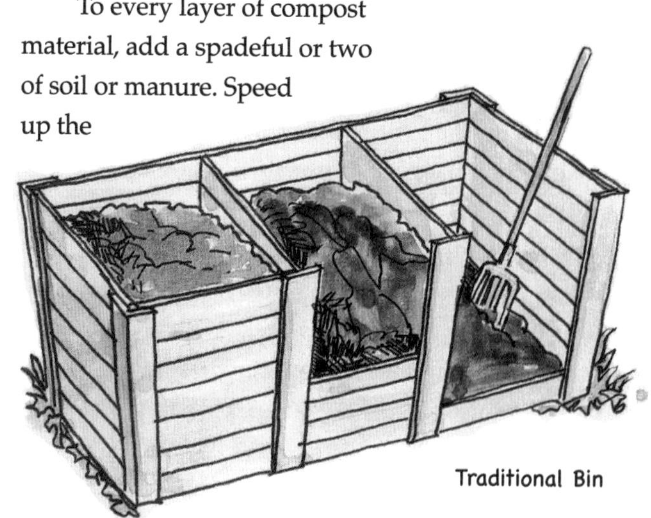

Traditional Bin

compost process with one of the commercially available compost accelerators, regular applications of manure, seaweed or seaweed extracts, or compost herbs. Borage, comfrey, chamomile, dandelion, or yarrow all speed up the process. Grow some near the bin and throw in a few leaves whenever you think of it. The ordinary stinging nettle will also work wonders and often grows as a weed—cut or pull some (wearing gloves to protect your hands) and put into the compost bin.

Seaweed, if available, or seaweed extract can be used as an accelerator too, as well as manures and organic fertilizers such as blood and bone.

Compost must be moist but not wet to compost actively. Put a cover over your container—a sheet of heavy duty plastic or even a sheet of corrugated iron—to keep rain from leaching the heap.

It is important to keep air circulating through your heap, so fork it over a couple of times a week, or use a "compost aerator," which is simply a barbed spike on a long handle which you drive deep into the pile, twist, and lift out. The barbs catch material as you lift it out, allowing more air into the center of the pile. It's easier work than forking.

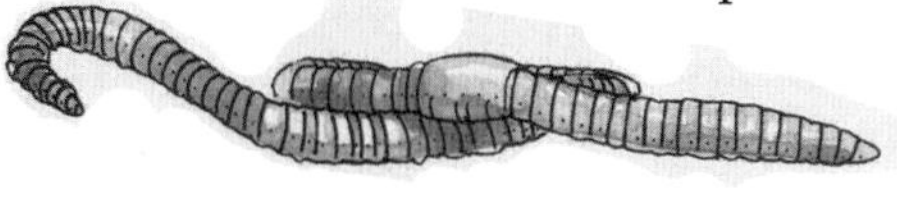

The compost should heat up, and in summer in a warm climate you may even see it steaming at times. In these conditions, you could expect usable compost in just six weeks. In temperate areas, the process will take longer—about three months.

A good, healthy compost heap should not smell. Bad smells could be a sign that the pile is too wet—leave it uncovered on fine days to evaporate the excess moisture and sprinkle over half a cup of lime or dolomite. A handful of chamomile added occasionally will also help keep it sweet.

Never put any food scraps—particularly meat or bones—into your heap, as this will attract rats, mice, cockroaches, maggots, and the local dogs.

The lower part of your heap will be full of earthworms that work away feeding on the compost and turning it into rich soil.

If you don't think you have enough worms, you can buy some from a worm farm and put them gently into the composted part of the heap where they won't be at risk of burning. Remember that they are quite delicate creatures and can be killed by contact with fertilizers.

When your compost is dark and friable, it is ready to use. Start mining it from the bottom of the heap and dig it into the garden. You can use it as potting soil, alone or mixed with commercial potting mix, or as a mulch.

If you prefer, there are ready-made compost bins available. Allowing for good drainage, it can be placed anywhere convenient. You simply remove the top and put in your biodegradable scraps, leaves, etc. The bottom of the bin is open to the soil for easy access of earthworms. Once the compost is complete, the bin can be easily lifted leaving the compost-cake ready for use.

Watering Techniques

Trench or furrow irrigation is often used in vegetable gardens. To avoid erosion of the soil, place a board under the hose when filling the trench.

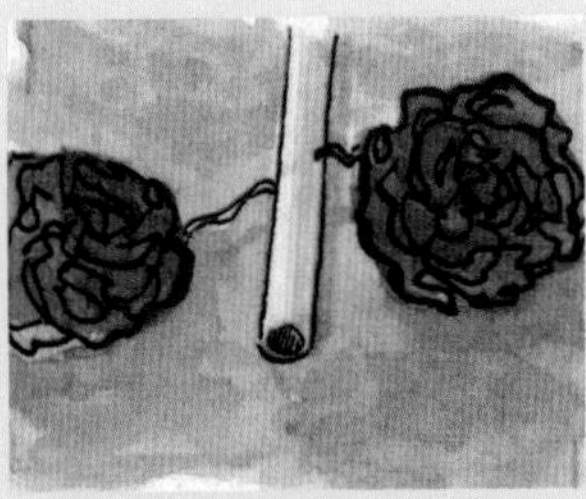

Drip watering carries the water to each plant.

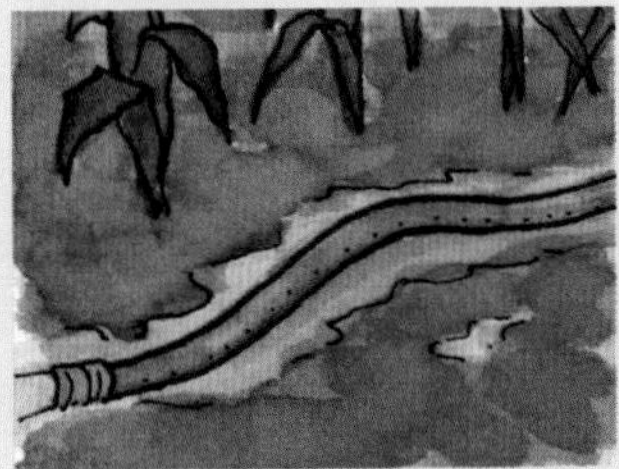

Quick Drip Punch holes in a tin can or hose for a simple drip system

An **Impulse Sprinkler** works anywhere in the garden. However, it must be high enough to ensure the water reaches over all the plants.

Watering the Garden

Watering can be time-consuming, so the five-minute gardener will need to install a watering system. DIY kits are available from nurseries and hardware stores and are simple and quick to install. For vegetables, choose a dripper system so that water is delivered to the soil rather than spraying over the foliage of plants. Constant wetting of foliage will encourage mildew in susceptible plants such as pumpkin, cucumber, and melons.

A timer is a further time-saver; you needn't spend any of your five minutes watering. But you do need to experiment to work out a suitable length of watering time. Dial up 15 minutes of water then check that the water has penetrated to make the soil at root level damp. If not, set the dial for further five-minute increments until you've worked out the optimum watering time for your garden. Now you can set and forget.

Using a watering system saves water as well as time. The water is directed so that there is no wasteful run-off or evaporation. Timers often indicate gallon or liter flow per minute, allowing you to calculate the exact amount of water being used. This is important if you depend on tank water.

Don't turn on the water automatically. Always check the soil first to see if it is dry. Allowing the soil time to dry between waterings is important as it helps control the spread of fungal diseases, which multiply quickly in moist conditions.

Deep watering two or three times a week will encourage plant roots to grow down deeper and produce good, even growth. Light daily sprinkling, on the other hand, only wets the top inch (2cm) of soil and encourages the roots to come to the surface in the search for water. Shallow-rooted plants wilt quickly and grow slowly.

Early morning is the best time to water. Plants and soil watered early have time to dry during the day and are not left wet and fungus-prone overnight.

Except in very hot, dry periods and in gardens with sandy soil, you won't need to water daily, provided the beds are well mulched. Germinating seed, young seedlings, and new transplants will need more frequent watering than established plants. Keep a watering can filled with water handy so that these can be given extra watering at times when you are not turning on the watering system.

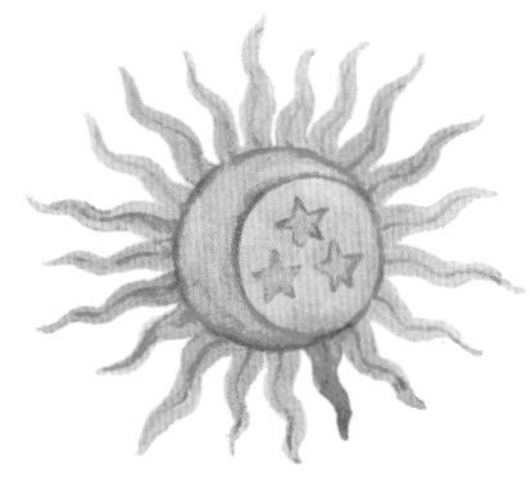

The glory of gardening:
hands in the dirt, head in the sun,
heart with nature. To nurture a garden
is to feed not just on the body,
but the soul.

~Alfred Austin

chapter 3

Vegetables

Planning a Five-Minute Vegetable Garden

Congratulations on deciding to become a five-minute vegetable gardener. Your first task is to work out the best place to spend your five minutes. Convention tells us that vegetable gardens come in rectangular plots up the back of backyards, but this needn't be the case. Your five-minute vegetable garden simply needs to be in a place with lots of sun—six hours is the recommended daily dose. The other vegetable requirements of good soil and regular water can be supplied by you. Only nature can turn on the sun.

Look carefully at your garden to see which part of it gets full sun each day. Morning sun is especially important as it

stimulates the growth pattern of plants. Plants rest during the hours of darkness and become active as soon as the sun shines on them. Sunlight triggers the green cells in their leaves to begin converting light to the sugars and starches, which are essential to plant growth. At the other end of the plant, the sun warms the soil, which stimulates root activity.

Vegetables that are shaded all morning then blasted by full afternoon sun will languish because they have a long inactive period from dusk till around mid-day or even later the following day. This can add up to 18 hours when plants aren't in active growth because of shade and cold soil. Following this long resting period with six hours of punishing heat amounts to cruelty and never amounts to good vegetables.

The key to a productive garden for the five-minute vegetable gardener is to find the best place to grow the vegetables, wherever that might be.

Amongst Flowers

The essential requirement for vegetables is sunshine, so for gardeners with cool and shady backyards, the sunny front garden might be the only option. But that doesn't mean giving up flowers. For centuries clever gardeners have used the ornamental aspects of vegetables to make beautiful and delicious gardens. There are plenty of vegetables that combine well with flowers, and your flowers will appreciate the good soil treatment, and the regular watering and feeding program that is part of the five-minute vegetable gardener's routine.

You could start simply with a vegetable edging on an existing flower bed. Small lettuce varieties such as mignonette, loose-growing salad leaves such as corn salad, the lacy leaves of mizuna, baby beets, ferny baby carrot tops, and Tiny Tim tomatoes all make attractive borders. Think about herbs too—an edge of silvery sage or the frizzy curls of bright green parsley or the lime green mounds of globe basil would all add to your kitchen as well as to your garden.

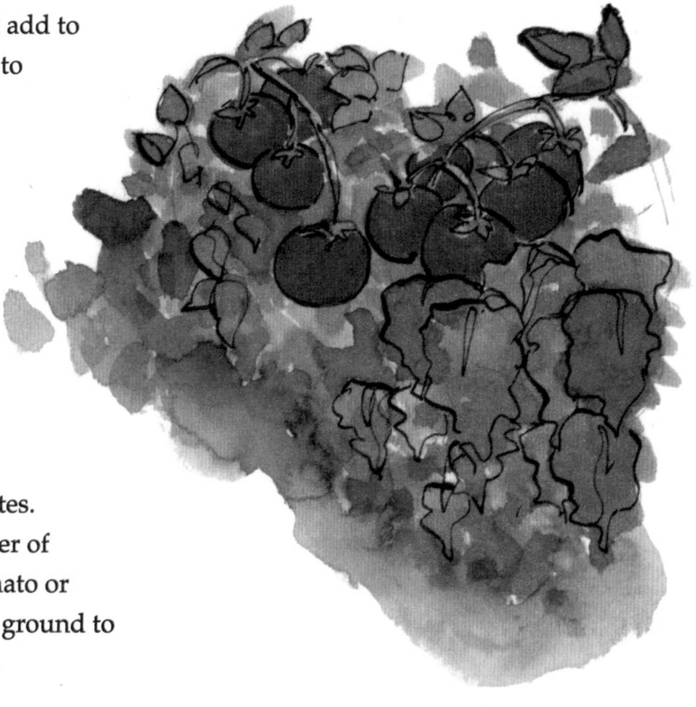

In amongst the flowers lend some height with a planting of Scarlet Runner beans. These have large fragrant scarlet flowers much prized by veggie gardeners in cool climates. Select a spot in the center of the bed, push three tomato or bamboo stakes into the ground to

Runner Beans

Gardeners in temperate and tropical climates shouldn't bother with the pretty Scarlet Runner beans on a tripod in the flower bed or up a pergola or along a fence: the Scarlet Runner bean is successful only in cool climates.

form a tripod, wind string around it for extra support and plant your beans. This is quick and easy.

Gardeners in warm and subtropical areas, though, can experiment with hibiscus plants dotted amongst the ornamental shrubs.

Foliage plants are important accents for the flower bed and needn't just add nuances of green. Among the herbs, bronze fennel and purple sage stand out for their distinctive foliage while the colored stems of rhubarb and red-stemmed Swiss chard make good choices. Striking in an all-white garden is the globe artichoke, with its thistle-like silver foliage growing tall in the back row of an herbaceous border. Broad beans, with their white flowers marked with chocolate brown, look great in a tumble along a white picket fence.

Some vegetables will do your flowers extra favors by warding away pests. A circle of leeks or onions around standard roses should keep away the aphids, for example, as well as look attractive against the flowers.

In Pots

Just because your gardening is confined to balcony, patio, or courtyard, there's no reason to forgo growing a few vegetables. In fact, the convenience of pots is perfect for the five-minute gardener.

Vegetables can be just as attractive as flowering plants, particularly if you choose them with an eye for the decorative effect of foliage and fruit. Tomatoes and peppers come high on the list, making handsome container plants grown on a sunny patio. They're just as colorful as a tub of geraniums and they certainly taste better. There are dwarf varieties of tomato available, such as Sweet 100, Tumbler

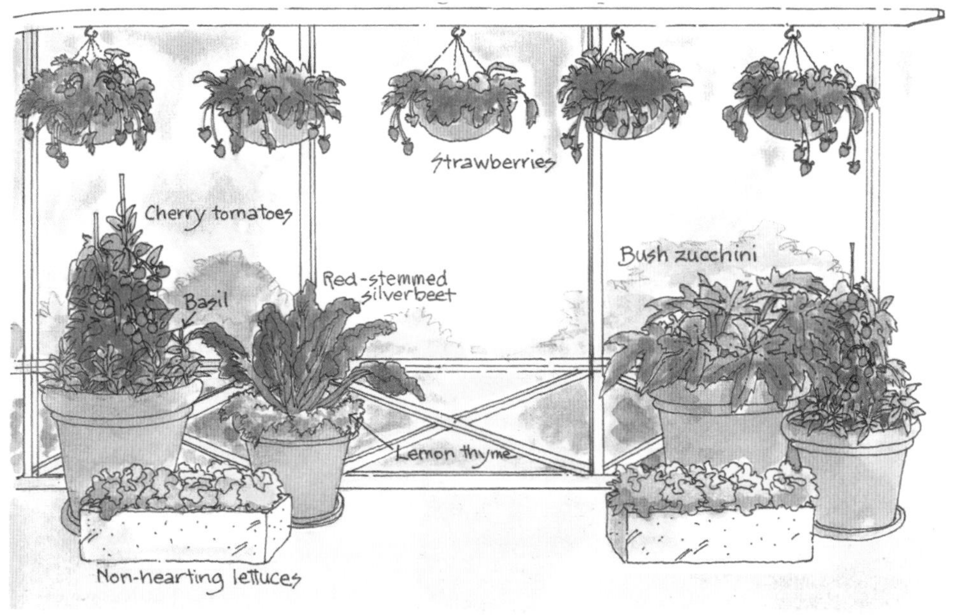

Hybrid, and others, which are ideal for the balcony gardener. They can be grown in a pot or hanging basket in any sunny space.

Pot gardeners shouldn't overlook the taller growing tomatoes, though. These give a more substantial result and can make a great visual impact, especially those varieties which carry a great crop of clusters of small, brightly colored fruit. Look for Sweet 100 and Yellow Canary.

Plant tomatoes in a tub with a stake at the back of the plant and give them a regular grooming by trimming off dead leaves and keeping them trained neatly up the stake. Spray with pyrethrum to control aphids and use Safer Caterpillar Killer to control caterpillars so that the plants always look their best.

Peppers and chilies are also bright additions to the courtyard garden with their shiny fruits in red, green, or yellow. A cluster of potted peppers grouped together on a balcony or courtyard can add long-lasting color when

Easiest of all for the five-minute pot gardener are all the leafy open-hearted lettuces, such as Red Salad Bowl and Buttercrunch, and the salad leaf crops, such as Corn Salad. They'll grow well in the polystyrene boxes you can pick up from your greengrocer. Pick a few leaves a time to make a salad of great variety.

most of summer's flowers are finished. Some of the eggplants are very decorative too. Easter Egg has fruit in several colors, for example, and Florentine Silk is purple and white. More aesthetic interest as well as kitchen produce can be added with the strong stem color of beets and rhubarb and the cherry translucency of red-stemmed Swiss chard.

Shallots, radish, and senposai, a Japanese green which can be cooked like spinach or used like lettuce and is ready for harvesting a speedy five weeks from sowing, are all good choices for potted gardeners.

But you needn't contain yourself to traditional plot vegetables. Plant hybridists, always on the lookout for a new market, have developed a number of vegetables especially for growing in containers. Look for Baby carrot, Pot Luck cucumber, Jack Be Little pumpkin, Blackjack lettuce, and Golden zucchini.

When growing vegetables in pots, give them a good start with three parts good potting mix combined with one part compost or old manure. The organic material will aid the water-holding capacity of the soil. Don't fiddle around with little containers. Use pots that are big enough to make an impression, both on the patio and in the kitchen. A tub featuring a tall-growing tomato might be edged with a loose-leafed lettuce, basil, or radish. Or an urn sprouting Swiss chard could have strawberries trailing from its sides.

On the Windowsill

Some gardeners don't even have a courtyard in which to grow vegetables. The most must be made of sunny windowsills and balconies. For this purpose, mustard and cress are a first choice. They can be grown in small baskets, and make little demand on the gardener—they can even be grown on a damp cloth! Snip off a harvest as soon as the plants have developed a true pair of leaves. Scatter the tiny leaves in salads, use them to add bite to a homemade mayonnaise, or pile them on freshly buttered bread.

Small pots of culinary herbs such as parsley, basil, chives, coriander, and mint can be grown on a bright windowsill.

Ideal for the cook, such an arrangement isn't ideal for the plants. They will be short-lived. Replaced often, though, they'll provide a garden-less cook with reliable and handy access to fresh herbs.

The dwarf and small tomatoes, such as Sweet 100, will also grow well on a sunny windowsill. Being self-pollinating, the only things tomatoes need to fruit well is enough light and enough water.

Another option for the salad bowl is to grow sprouts. Several varieties are available in seed packets. They can be grown in a jar by the kitchen sink and only need rinsing twice a day in clean water. This will encourage them to sprout and they'll be ready to eat in a few days.

For gardeners with not even a sunny windowsill to call their own, the solution is mushrooms.

A mushroom farm is available from nurseries through most of the year, but as different varieties are grown at different times of the year, make sure you choose one that is suitable for the season.

As well as the usual "field" mushroom, it is now also possible to find more unusual varieties, such as the Asian Shitake mushroom.

Keep your mushroom farm in a cupboard, under the stairs or on a shady balcony and give it regular watering. It will reward you with a huge crop of safe-to-eat, delicious mushrooms.

Once you've polished off your harvest, pass the spent compost onto a gardening friend.

To save on water and help protect your plants through the worst of summer, look for the new potting mixes specially designed to retain water—they really work. A handful of water-saving granules mixed in before planting will also help prevent soil drying out in hot and windy weather.

Strawberries are a good choice for the five-minute container gardener. They make charming patio plants if you can beat the birds. Grow them in hanging baskets as well as troughs and the traditional strawberry pots. They'll appreciate a little more shade than other vegetables, which is another bonus for the small-space gardener.

Five minutes a day will give the small-space gardener plenty of time for a little puttering around—hand-picking pests and damaged leaves, feeding and watering, and simply enjoying the feeling of growing your own dinner.

Goodbye Lawn

Lawns often occupy the sunniest parts of the garden. If you are devoting your garden's supply of solar energy to growing grass, consider replacing some or most of the lawn with a much more productive crop—vegetables.

The five-minute gardener will want to do this the easy way. Instead of mattocks and hoes and back-breaking labor, the tools for this method are newspaper, a bale or two of straw or spoiled alfalfa hay, manure, and compost.

Start by choosing a sunny part of the lawn. Mark out the area that you want to convert to vegetables. Use the garden hose to do this, pulling the hose to mark out the required shape and size. Put a garden edging in place using treated pine, railway sleepers, or elegant terracotta edging tiles, if you can afford them.

Having edged your bed, spread newspaper all over it, to the thickness of about 20 pages, making sure the sections are well overlapped. Water to keep the paper in position as you work.

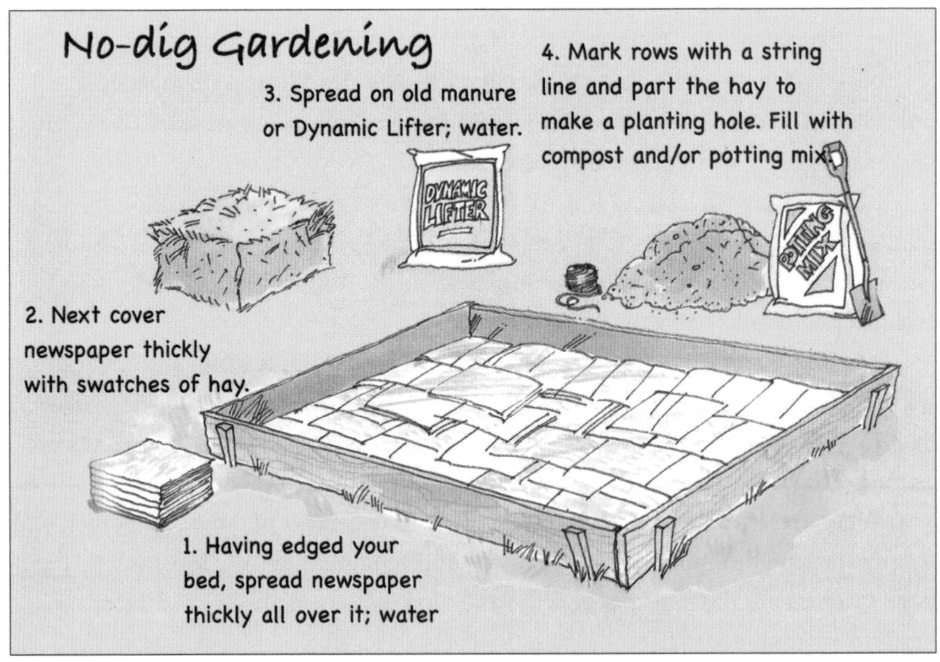

Potato First

It is popular gardener's folklore that the way to ensure a great new lawn is to first plant a crop of potatoes around your new house. Potatoes are credited with exerting some mystical effect on the soil, which guarantees gorgeous grass. In fact, the potato crop does help. Digging over the ground to harvest the crop improves aeration, the fertilizer used enriches the soil, and the surface mulch breaks down and gets the earthworms active. The subsequent grass goes down into improved conditions and you get to eat some healthy new potatoes.

Next cover the newspaper thickly 8–12 inches (20–30cm) with swatches pulled from a bale of hay. Over this spread a bag or two of old manure. Water this layer cake gently and you're ready to plant.

Mark rows with a string line for a neat bed and part the hay to make a planting hole. Fill it generously with compost (add potting mix to make a half-and-half blend if you don't have enough compost). Plant a seed or seedling in each prepared hole and water carefully.

The straw and manure will compost down as the plants grow and the roots will spread out into the compost. A dressing of blood and bone can be broadcast over the bed as the veggies grow. Add more straw or hay as a mulch if necessary as the season progresses.

When the crop has been harvested you'll have a layer of good soil, which you simply top up with more hay and manure and replant as before. Meanwhile, the lawn underneath the newspaper will have died off, having been cut off from the light for several months.

Ideas for the Backyard

The sunniest part of your garden may be the backyard. This is where most people consider the ideal vegetable garden should be. But where in the backyard?

If you've got a rotary clothesline in the backyard, chances are it's in the sunniest spot. So make the vegetable beds underneath it, leaving just enough space to stand and hang clothes on the line. Plant low-growing herbs and vegetables—you don't want tall growers such as sweet corn and tall tomatoes tangling with the sheets. The only drawback of the clothesline veggie patch is that you'll need to bring your washing in as soon as it's dry. The vegetables won't appreciate unnecessary hours of shade.

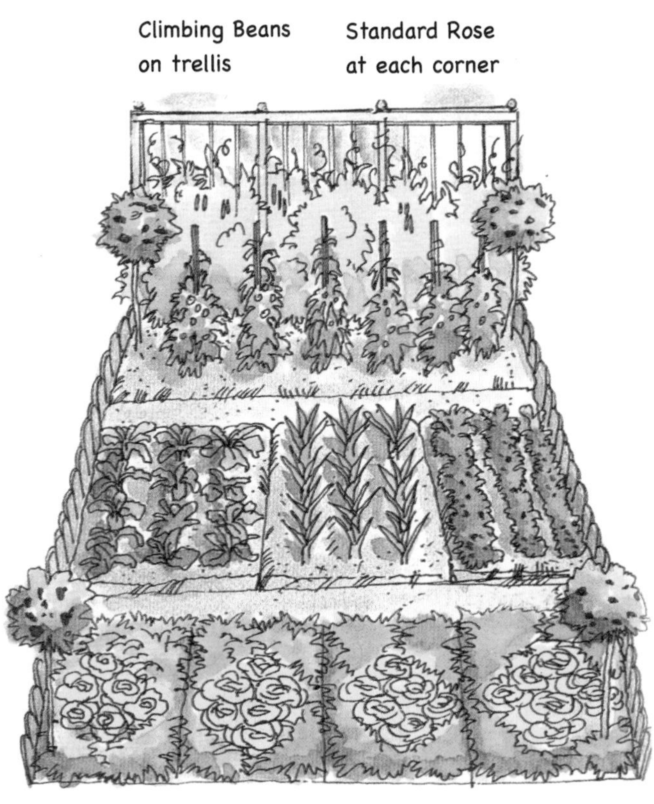

More conventional

is the rectangular vegetable garden of straight rows and neat paths, perhaps with a trellis on the southernmost side for beans or an espaliered fruit tree. Other tall growers should be planted on the southern side so that they don't shade smaller plants. Beds running on a north/south axis will get the full benefit of sun all day, but if this isn't possible, position the bed to get maximum sunlight hours.

Three bed garden

A satisfactory size for a new rectangular vegetable bed is 10 feet (3m) wide and 13 feet (4m) long. Divide it into three long beds with paths just wide enough to walk down. These will provide easy access to all plants. As your gardening skill or enthusiasm increases, you can add extra 3 feet (1m) wide beds to the basic patch.

Neat rows are certainly easiest for the five-minute vegetable gardener. Straight rows makes for quicker watering, fertilizing, and mulching. But generations of gardeners have found playing with pattern in the kitchen garden an irresistible temptation. A diamond of ferny carrots might be edged by triangles of red mignonette, for example, which makes a square that meets a chunk of red-stemmed Swiss chard.

Playing with color and form in the vegetable garden has led gardeners to look at different shapes for the whole bed. What about a giant vegetable pie, divided into slices by grass paths just wide enough for the mower. In the center, a sundial would give a classical feel to your garden.

Careful planning of your vegetable garden will give your plants an advantage and will also make your veggie garden pleasing to the eye. Once you've satisfied the vegetable good health requirements—rich soil, regular water, lots of sun—the design decisions and the variety decisions make vegetable gardening just as creative as any other kind of gardening.

Layout and Planting Schemes

Planning what to plant is the easiest job for the five-minute vegetable gardener. The only tools required are a piece of paper and a pencil, with a seed catalog or two. The question of what to plant will be answered immediately if you have a strong single reason for wanting a vegetable garden. It might be that you're sick of tomatoes that taste like cardboard, or that you want a steady supply of vegetable delicacies such as snow peas and asparagus.

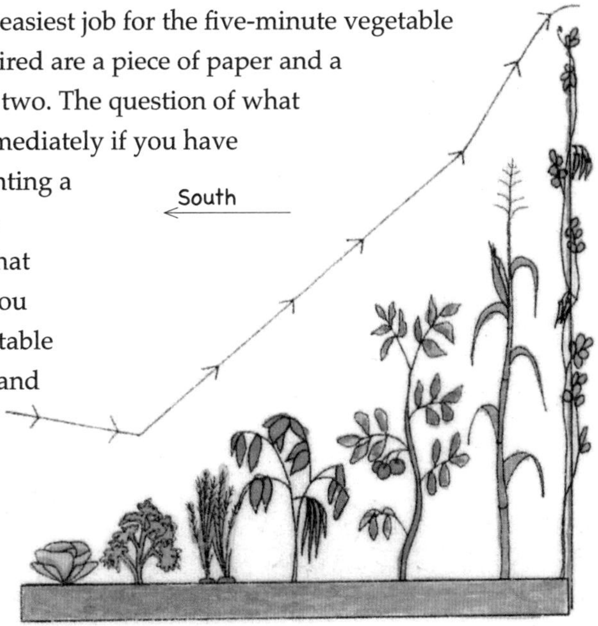

South

Maximizing sun angles and deflecting hot winds with a rising foliage slope.

You might have a philosophical bent towards biodiversity, believing that the monoculture of current agriculture methods is threatening the future of

To keep your feet dry and boots clean, cover the paths in your garden bed with a 3–4-inch (6–8cm) layer of straw, sawdust or even old carpet. This will save time on changing footwear before and after your five-minute sorties to the garden.

the planet. If so, your garden will be full of heirloom plants, the seeds of which have been saved by generations of home gardeners. These plants are usually reliable and disease-free, with natural selection having weeded out the weak. Their major difference to commercial varieties will be that they don't keep long enough to be trucked around the country, they don't pack easily into uniformly-sized trays, or they don't fit our often limited vision of what a vegetable "should" look like.

A Family Garden

When planning a vegetable garden for your family, the first rule is not to consider anything your family doesn't like to eat. Attempting vegetable conversion is just too stressful for the five-minute gardener. Choose firm favorites instead, with an eye to how your family likes to live. Salads all through summer, perhaps, replaced by thick veggie soups in winter.

You might also want to consider whole dishes or

favorite combinations and make sure you grow the ingredients you need. Coleslaw requires carrots and cabbage and is even better with chopped celery mixed through; spinach makes a great pie when mixed with lots of parsley and crumbled feta cheese; tomatoes like growing with basil and make a good pair on the plate, and

How Many Plants to Grow for a Veggie-Loving Family of Four			
Artichoke	3–6 plants	**Lettuce**	10–12 plants
Asparagus	20–25 plants	**Onion**	13 feet (4m) row
Beans, dwarf	10–13 feet (3–4m) row	**Shallots**	13 feet (4m) row
Beans, climbing	3–10 feet (1–3m) row	**Parsnip**	10 feet (3m) row
Beans, broad	17–20 feet (5–6m) row	**Peas, dwarf**	10–17 feet (3–5m) row
Beets	7 feet (2m) row	**Peas, climbing**	3–7 feet (1–2m) row
Broccoli	10 plants	**Peppers**	6–8 plants
Brussels sprouts	6–10 plants	**Potatoes**	20–24 plants
Cabbage	9–12 plants	**Pumpkin**	6 plants
Chinese cabbage	6–9 plants	**Radish**	3 feet (1m) row
Cauliflower	6–12 plants	**Rhubarb**	6 plants
Carrots	13 feet (4m) row	**Spinach**	12 plants
Celery	15–20 plants	**Sweet Corn**	24 plants
Chayote	2 plants	**Swiss chard**	12 plants
Chili	1 plant	**Strawberry**	10–15 plants
Cucumber	6 plants	**Tomatoes**	10–15 plants
Eggplant	4–6 plants	**Turnips**	10 feet (3m) row
Leeks	3–7 feet (1–2m) row	**Zucchini**	6 plants

The Summer Family Plot

This plan for a summer vegetable plot is designed for a family of four, who love eating out during the warm months and whose staple summer diet includes barbecues with lots of green salads and pastas with vegetable sauces. Successive plantings mean a longer harvest time.

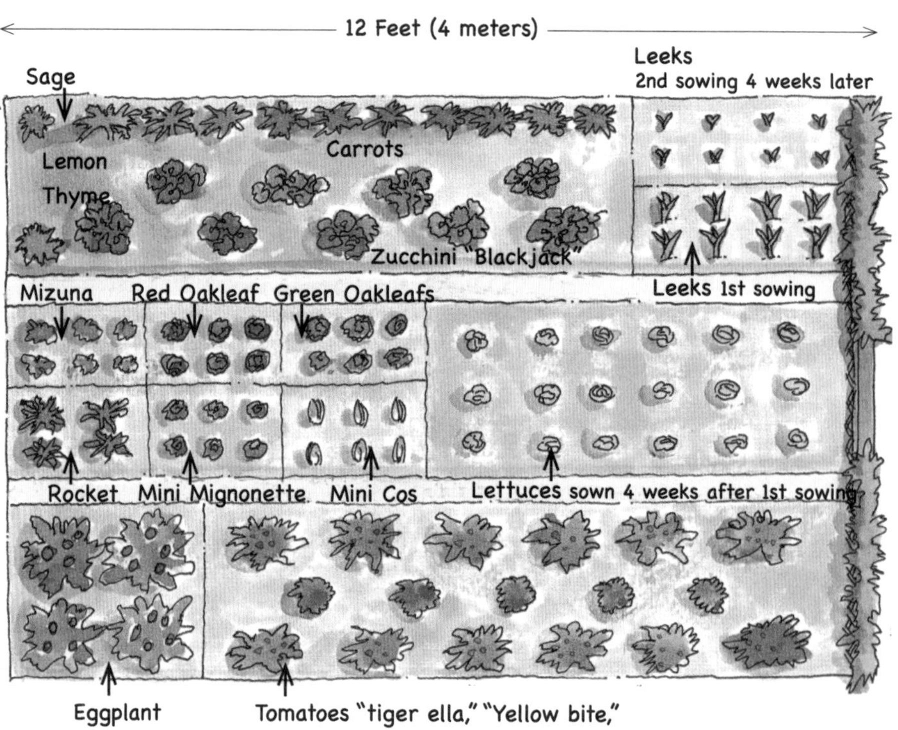

The Winter Family Plot

If you live in a warmer climate, try this plan for a winter garden. Fresh-from-the-garden produce is always much better than its store-bought counterpart, and you'll be pleased to know that your winter vegetables often have a higher vitamin content and are tastier than the supermarket vegetables that sometimes do not take shipping well.

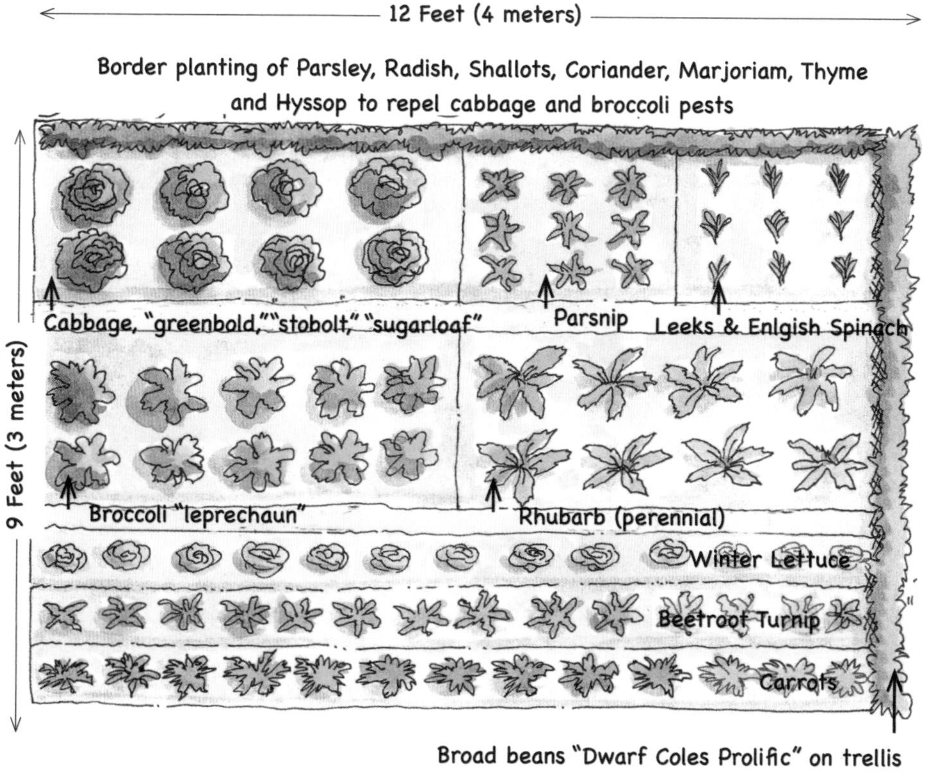

12 Feet (4 meters)

Border planting of Parsley, Radish, Shallots, Coriander, Marjoriam, Thyme and Hyssop to repel cabbage and broccoli pests

9 Feet (3 meters)

Cabbage, "greenbold," "stobolt," "sugarloaf"

Parsnip

Leeks & Enlgish Spinach

Broccoli "leprechaun"

Rhubarb (perennial)

Winter Lettuce

Beetroot Turnip

Carrots

Broad beans "Dwarf Coles Prolific" on trellis

the basil can be turned into pesto with the addition of parsley, pine nuts, parmesan, and garlic; ratatouille is good served with meat or as a pasta sauce and requires from your garden eggplant, leek, zucchini, peppers, and tomatoes; and beans make a lovely salad dressed with chopped dill and walnuts.

Experience will teach you how many plants you need to satisfy your family's appetite so you don't end up growing gluts that you must beg friends and relatives to take off your hands. If you're just starting out, follow the recommendations in this chart on pg. 45, which is based on the veggie-loving habits of a family of four.

When growing cauliflower for the family, choose three different varieties that mature at different times.

Planting to Save Space

The five-minute vegetable gardener will be looking for the highest yield from the least space. Follow these tips to maximize the effects of your effort.

1. Grow small, compact varieties. There are many vegetables that have been developed to answer the demand for smaller-sized plants.

These include lettuce, carrot, and cauliflower and some of the notorious ramblers, such as cucumber, pumpkin, and melon. Many of the small versions of these plants will even grow in containers. Look for bush zucchini, bush pumpkins, and small-sized watermelon. All have a bushy, non-runner form and take up far less room than their parents. The fruits of these plants are often smaller than the originals as well, which is not a drawback for the small family.

2. Use every available sunny space by filling foam boxes with compost and potting mix and planting with a crop of mixed lettuce, Tiny Tim tomatoes, baby carrot, radish, and mixed herbs.
3. Don't ignore the potential of vertical space. Grow climbing vegetables on a tripod, a cylinder of wire mesh, a trellis against a sunny fence, or in window boxes or hanging baskets.
4. Concentrate on quick-growing crops that won't occupy the ground too long—potatoes, for instance, take a long time and

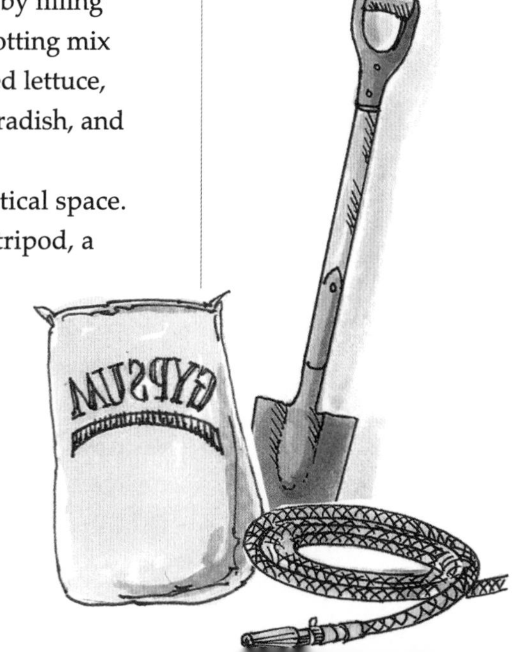

need a lot of space. High-yield-for-space favorites include lettuces, tomatoes, beans, peas, and herbs.

Planting to Save Money

There are all kinds of reasons for a five-minute gardener to become a five-minute veggie gardener and economy is just one. But to save money from your five-minute gardening you will need to consider your plantings carefully. If saving cents is the aim, it makes little sense to grow onions, for example, which are cheap to buy, store easily (and don't take up room in the fridge), are always available, and take time and effort to grow. On the other hand, leeks are expensive, availability is variable but the gardening input is no more arduous than for onions.

Lettuce is one of the best money-saving choices for the five-minute veggie gardener. They're pricey, don't store very well, and if you like variety in your salad bowl, will take up most of the space in your fridge crisper. For the gardener, though, lettuce is easy to grow and can be harvested a few leaves at a time, fresh for that evening's salad. Add tomatoes, which fetch premium prices for real taste, and you will be knocking dollars off your supermarket bill.

Consider these money-saving principles too:

1. Don't waste time with a plant that is not giving a good return in your garden. If something doesn't grow unless it is constantly sprayed and cosseted, get rid of it and grow something reliable for your particular situation. Select varieties that suit your climate, soil, and space. Look for vegetables that are resistant to virus or fungal disease (read the packet before purchasing to check).
2. Remember that the only thing that positively enjoys shade is mint, so don't waste time, money, and energy trying to grow vegetables in anything but full sun.
3. Don't grow a crop your family doesn't enjoy eating—throwing uneaten greens into the compost is not an economy.
4. If you have a friend or neighbor growing veggies, try to coordinate your crops—you grow tomatoes while he grows lettuce; if he's got pumpkin, you put in potatoes—and share the bounty.
5. Remember the basic law of veggie gardening—no matter what you grow, there

Fine seed that is just covered can dry out quickly. Instead of covering with soil, sprinkle a thin layer of vermiculite, which is available from nurseries in small bags, along the rows. This is very light, but retains moisture so that seed does not dry out. Tiny germinating seeds can also push through the covering easily. The trail of vermiculite makes it easy to see just where you planted the seeds.

will inevitably be a glut of it in the shops just when you are ready to harvest a bumper crop.

Planting

It's important to grow your vegetables at the right time of year. Vegetables planted at the wrong time will bolt (go to seed without developing properly). Some vegetables, such as lettuce and onion, are particularly sensitive to planting time and different varieties are available for planting at different times of the year. Follow the guidelines in this book before sowing seed, and read the back of the seed packet carefully. This will tell you the time of year to plant, recommended spacing and planting depth and time to harvest.

Most vegetables can be sown from seed directly into the rows where they are to grow. By planting out advanced seedlings from a nursery, however, you will save about six weeks growing

time. If the soil is dry the night before you plan to plant, water it so that it will be damp-dark when you start work. Before planting, rake the soil until it is fine, smooth, and even. Use a string line or a length of timber to mark the rows, then draw a stick or the corner of the hoe along the guide, leaving a shallow furrow an inch (2–3cm) deep.

Seed is dropped into the furrow and covered. As seeds are planted at varying depths, check your seed packet and cover lightly or liberally as required. Some seeds, such as peas and beans, can be pushed down a little to the required depth.

After planting, water very gently using a watering can with a fine spout, or the hose set on its finest spray. Take care that the seed is not disturbed. Keep soil damp until seeds germinate. If the seedbeds dry out for even a short period at germination time, the plants will be lost. Lettuce is very sensitive to drying out at germination time and this is a common cause of failure with lettuce seed.

It is important to mulch your bed after planting. Mulch can be spread between the rows of vegetables to a depth of at least three inches (8cm). If your vegetables are planted in straight rows, it is very quick to do this. Mulching will keep the weeds down (the five-minute vegetable gardener doesn't have time to spend in removing any more than the odd weed). Mulch will also keep soil moisture from being evaporated during hot weather and will keep the soil warmer in winter.

Mulch can be anything organic. Choose from leaves, mulch from a mulch machine, composted lawn clippings, seaweed (an excellent choice for sandy seaside gardens), pea straw, spoiled alfalfa hay, straw, or other regional products such as nutshells or rice hulls.

Spring Plantings

- • after frosts
- •• raise early plants in pots
- ••• early in the season only
- •••• late in the season

Cool Climate		
Artichoke (shoots) •••	Cauliflower •	Peas •••
Beans (climbing) •••	Cucumber ••	Potato
Beans (dwarf) •••	Eggplant •	Pumpkin ••
Beets	Garlic cloves	Radish
Broccoli •	Herbs	Squash ••
Brussels sprouts•	Leek •	Sweet corn •
Cabbage	Lettuce	Swiss chard
Carrots	Marrow •	Tomato
Celery	Melon ••	
Temperate Climate		
Beans (climbing) •••	Garlic cloves	Radish
Beans (dwarf) •••	Herbs	Rhubarb
Beets	Leek	Scallions
Cabbage	Lettuce	Squash ••
Carrots	Marrow ••	Sweet Corn
Celery	Melon ••	Swiss chard
Chayote •••	Parsnip	Tomato
Cucumber ••	Potato •••	
Eggplant	Pumpkin ••	
Tropical climate		
Beans (climbing) •••	Cucumber	Radish
Beans (dwarf) •••	Eggplant	Scallions
Beets •••	Lettuce	Squash
Cabbage	Marrow	Sweet corn
Carrots	Melons	Swiss chard
Chayote •••	Pumpkin	Tomatoes

In hot weather or if the soil is light and sandy, cover the seedbed with damp newspaper or damp burlap until plants begin to germinate. After a few days, start lifting the cover to check for germinating plants and as soon as the seeds start coming through, remove the cover.

A Year in the Five-Minute Vegetable Garden

Spring

Spring is a rewarding time to plant a vegetable garden because everything grows quickly in the warming soils and longer days. Many people love salads, as they remind them of those long hot days of summer. You can enjoy the sense of summer early by planting salad vegetables in spring. The non-hearting lettuces are especially easy to grow, but choose from peppers, carrot, celery, cucumber, radish, shallot, and tomato to complement your platter of salad greens. These are all medium to small growers.

If your family loves coleslaw, try some small, early cabbage varieties that mature in eight weeks, such as Harvester Queen. Chinese cabbage is also quick growing, with a delicate flavor and tender texture. It may bolt in hot weather, though, so keep it growing quickly and use it young.

Add popular salad herbs such as basil, chives, coriander, marjoram, parsley, and mint to spring meals. Grow them as garden edgings or in troughs.

As the weather begins to warm and your vegetables and other greenery in the garden begin to shoot and grow, a whole lot insects take it as in open

If in doubt about the safety of an insecticide, read the contents on the label carefully before buying or using.

invitation to a feast. Sucking and chewing insects have been over-wintering in egg form or as over-wintering adults (often on weeds) and they begin to emerge in the warmth and multiply to keep pace with the amount of food (your vegetables) available.

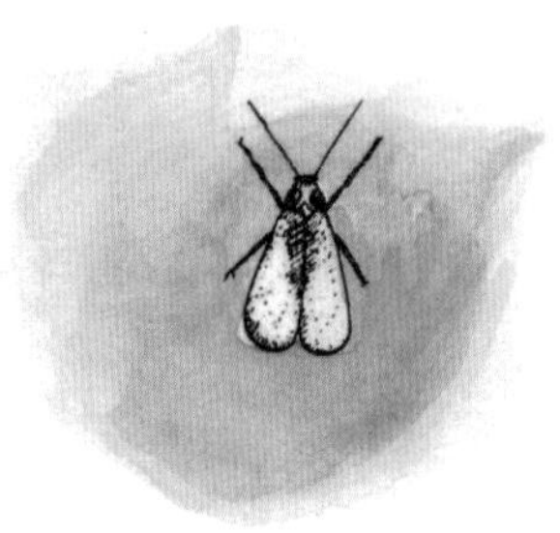

As the plants grow bigger by the day so does the insect population. It is important to control these insects right from the start as they carry diseases that they spread through the plant population.

Protecting your plants from sucking and chewing insects (aphids, thrips, etc.) in early spring will save much time, work, and anguish later in the season when the virus diseases begin to show up and destroy your crop.

A good example of this is woodiness or bullet of passion fruit, a virus disease that appears as fruit matures but is caused earlier in the season by sucking and chewing insects such as aphids.

Early spraying, when insects are first noticed in small numbers, is crucial. Most sucking and chewing insects, such as aphids and caterpillars, can be controlled with "safe" insecticides such as pyrethrum or pyrethrum-based sprays and other low-toxicity sprays.

Caterpillars that hatch into moths or butterflies can be controlled by Safer Caterpillar Killer.

Derris Dust is another safe alternative and is popularly used to control the green caterpillars of the cabbage butterfly.

Soap-based sprays such as Safer are other alternatives for the home gardener in search of the soft option.

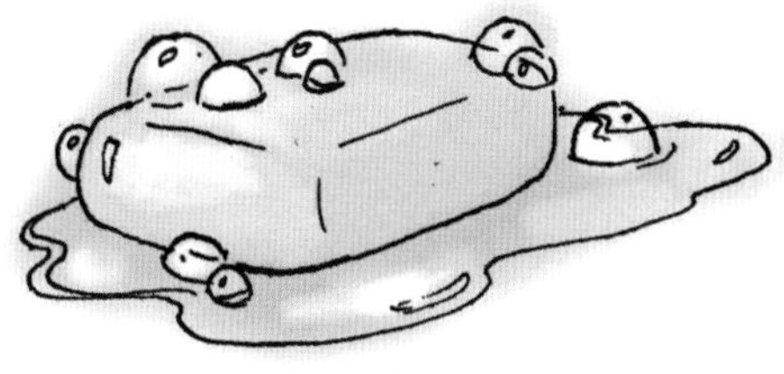

White oil is useful to combat scale insects, which it does by smothering them. It can also be used to make sprays "stick" on better and is often used with an insecticide to increase its effectiveness. Oil sprays should not be used in hot weather as it may damage the plants.

The five-minute gardener must take it into account that "friendly" sprays need to be used more frequently as they have a very short residual life, unlike chemical sprays that have a long-term effect. This means that "safe" spraying needs to be done more often and, therefore, is more time-consuming.

Mavrik is another useful spray for controlling insect pests such as aphids, thrips, and other soft-bodied pests.

Bugs and beetles with a hard shell and leaf miners, which are protected because they feed between the leaf

Subtropical gardeners should cover any empty beds with a thick layer of mulch as the wet season approaches. This will prevent the soil from washing away and will suppress weeds. Another option is to plant a green manure crop of lupins, barley, or mustard, which can be dug in to enrich the soil before the next planting.

surfaces, need to be sprayed with something more systemic like malathion.

One of the worst pests of the fruit and vegetable garden is the fruit fly and anyone in a fruit-fly area should be ready to spray this pest with an effective control.

In spring fruit fly attacks early-fruiting plants such as loquats. So spraying the fruit of these is essential if you hope to avoid a build-up of this destructive pest later in the season when your vegetables, such as tomatoes and peppers, will be attacked.

Fruit flies can be sprayed with carbaryl following the instructions on the container. Chemical baits can also be used and these are useful for tomatoes. These splash baits are not put directly onto the fruit but splashed on stakes, branches, leaves, nearby fences, and so on.

Lures such as plastic bottles with a bait (try honey, cider vinegar, or pieces of ripe banana) will trap fruit fly and, though it won't control them, will give a good idea of when numbers are building up and spraying should be done.

Summer

Summer is an exciting time in the garden because you'll be spending several of your five minutes picking the crop. When possible, pick in the cool of the morning, when the vegetables are fresh and crisp. Pick them young, small, and

The Five-Minute Vegetable Gardener on Holidays

Many people like to take their vacation during June and July, and if you're one of them you'll be abandoning your vegetable garden at a time when it is cropping well and needs regular attention.

Get ready for the holidays at least a month in advance with these steps:

1. Stop planting out new seeds or seedling that won't be able to survive without your care.
2. Mulch garden beds heavily to conserve soil moisture and keep weeds down.
3. Arrange for a friend or neighbor to come in about three times a week and turn on your watering system. Encourage them to pick and eat any maturing vegetables so that plants don't go to seed and fruit doesn't rot.

If you're at home but on holidays, lavish some extra care on your garden. Take the time to hitch up the trailer and visit a produce store for bales of straw or spoiled alfalfa hay to top up the mulch over your veggie beds. A stable or riding school in your area may also give away strawy stable manure, provided you can load it yourself. If you don't have a trailer, take a few large garbage bags and load up the trunk.

Work in the garden early in the morning and in the cool of the evening and always wear a hat and sunscreen. Avoid doing anything in the heat of the day, including spraying insecticide or fungicide, which will burn the foliage.

Summer Plantings

- • after frosts
- •• raise early plants in pots
- ••• early in the season only
- •••• late in the season

COOL CLIMATE		
Beans (climbing) •••	Cucumber	Radish
Beans (dwarf) •••	Eggplant •••	Rhubarb
Beets	Leeks	Scallions
Broccoli	Lettuce	Squash
Brussels sprouts	Marrow	Sweet corn
Cabbage	Melons	Swiss chard
Carrots	Parsnip	Tomatoes •••
Cauliflower	Potato	
Celery	Pumpkin	
TEMPERATE CLIMATE		
Beans (climbing)	Celery	Pumpkin •••
Beans (dwarf)	Cucumber	Radish
Beets	Eggplant	Rhubarb
Broccoli ••••	Leeks	Scallions
Brussels sprouts ••••	Lettuce	Squash
Cabbage	Marrow	Sweet corn
Carrots	Melons	Swiss chard
Cauliflower ••••	Parsnip	Tomatoes •••
TROPICAL CLIMATE		
Artichoke shoots ••••	Marrow	Squash
Cabbage	Melons	Sweet corn
Celery	Pumpkin	Swiss chard
Cucumber	Radish	Tomatoes
Eggplant	Rhubarb	
Lettuce	Scallions	

tender. Beans, for example, need to be picked every day or so, to prevent them aging into tough, stringy things. The more you pick beans the better, as all annual plants, such as peas and beans, zucchini and cucumber, will keep on producing as long as they aren't allowed to set seed.

Pick tomatoes frequently too. This makes them less likely to be attacked by fruit fly. Picked when pink, they can be ripened on the windowsill or in a brown paper bag with a banana or apple. Always pick anything that is likely to ripen in the next few days before you use any chemical sprays.

Insect activity is high in summer, with fruit flies, aphids, whitefly, caterpillars, bugs, and many other sucking and chewing insects at the frenzied peak of their activity. Keep them under control with regular applications of Derris Dust or Safer Caterpillar Killer on all members of the cabbage family. Check foliage and spray any unwelcome guests with pyrethrum before they have time to multiply.

Fungal diseases, which you'll notice as leaf spotting, fruit or root rot, are most likely to occur in the warm humid weather of summer. Keep your garden well mulched to prevent fungal spores in the soil from being splashed up onto stems and leaves.

Pick green tomatoes and use them for green tomato chutney. If there are lots of tomatoes still to ripen on the bushes, pull up the entire plant and hang it in a warm, dry shed. If the conditions are suitable, the tomatoes will continue to ripen.

A careful walk though your garden each day should allow you to spot disease early. Spray with a fungicide.

Carry a plastic bag with you in your basket during summer so that you can pull off any diseased leaves or fruits. Put the plastic bag straight in the bin. This will often prevent the disease from spreading. A sick plant should be pulled up and disposed of in the same way. Fallen fruit also needs to be picked up and thrown away. Never leave vegetables to rot on the ground—they will spread disease from fungal spores, which continue to grow. As well, insect pests such as fruit fly can go on breeding in rotting fruit and vegetables. Fruit fly-infested fruit should be put in a plastic bag and left in the hot sun for a couple of days to kill off the maggots, before being thrown away.

In cool areas, do not plant peas if they will be in flower when frosts are likely.

In warm to temperate climates you can continue making fresh plantings through summer. Plant beans, beets, carrots, Chinese cabbage, cucumber, lettuce, peppers, radish, scallions, sweet corn, Swiss chard, and tomatoes.

In cool areas, begin to plant brussels sprouts, broccoli, and cauliflower towards the end of summer.

In subtropical climates, slow down your planting as the wet

season approaches. Trying to cope with a vegetable garden in a wet season in just five minutes a day is a struggle as plants are damaged by heavy rain and prone to disease.

Autumn

As late summer turns into autumn, your summer veggies will be coming to an end. Pick any remaining vegetables and pull out plants as they become weak. Don't waste time spraying vegetables coming to the end of their season. Pull them up and put them into the compost or into the garbage bin if they are diseased.

It is important to continue collecting any rotting fruit and destroying it. Seal it tightly in a plastic bag and leave it in the hot sun for a day or two before putting it in the bin. Fruit fly-infested fruit and vegetables may also be burned.

Autumn is change-over time and the five-minute gardener will need to decide what to plant for the coming season. Many five-minute gardeners find their enthusiasm wanes with the end of the lush summer crops. If you want to take an

In southern areas, remember that germination takes longer in cool winter temperatures than during warmer weather, so allow a bit longer for seeds to come up. If you can provide bottom heat in a greenhouse or propagation box, germination will be more even and faster.

In frosty districts cover plants at night when frosts are expected. Recycle plastic juice bottles by cutting off the base to leave a "cloche" with a convenient handle for picking up and for storing when not in use.

Autumn Plantings

• after frosts
•• raise early plants in pots
••• early in the season only
•••• late in the season

Cool Climate		
Cabbage Leeks Lettuce	Onions •••• Radish ••• Scallions •••	Spinach Turnips •••
Temperate Climate		
Artichoke shoots •••• Beets ••• Broad bean •••• Broccoli Brussels sprouts •••• Cabbage Carrots •••	Cauliflower ••• Leeks Lettuce Onions Parsnip Peas (climbing) Peas (dwarf)	Radish Scallions Spinach Swiss chard ••• Turnips
Subtropical climate		
Artichoke shoots ••• Beans (climbing) Beans (dwarf) Beets Broad beans •••• Broccoli Cabbage Carrots Cauliflower	Celery Cucumber Eggplant Lettuce Marrow Melons Onions Parsnip Peas (climbing)	Peas (dwarf) Potato tubers Radish Scallions Spinach Squash Sweet corn Swiss chard Tomatoes

extra few minutes snuggled down under the covers on cold mornings, you can decide to slow down the production line.

It is a good idea to rest at least some of your vegetable beds. Resting vegetable beds can be liberally covered with manure, compost, and straw. This can be left to compost down through winter. It will be ready to replant in early spring. Alternatively you can plant the beds with green manure crops, such as winter cereals or lupin, which is left to growing until flowering time then chopped down and dug into the soil.

If you do decide to go ahead with new plantings, you can choose from the entire cabbage family, turnip, radish, winter-season onions, broad beans, beets,

Going Cold on Gardening

Some five-minute vegetable gardeners may not want to bother much with a winter veggie garden, but there are still things that should be done through these months to keep your garden in good condition ready for spring planting.

- Tidy up the veggie growing area and put any old pots and other rubbish into the bin. These are hiding places for snails, slugs, and other pests.
- Keep the area weeded. Do this quickly by chipping over with a Dutch hoe and covering the beds with a thick (3 inch/6–8cm) layer of mulch. Many gardeners will have a good supply of leaf mulch in winter after deciduous trees and shrubs have dropped their leaves and the summer's lawn clippings are nicely composted. The mulch will keep weeds down and will compost down over the cool months leaving a bed ready for spring plantings.
- If you don't expect to use your tools for a few months, make sure they are cleaned and oiled and put away tidily.

Winter Plantings

- • after frosts
- •• raise early plants in pots
- ••• early in the season only
- •••• late in the season

Cool Climate		
Artichoke shoots ••••	Lettuce	Peas (dwarf) •
Asparagus	Onions	Spinach
Broad beans	Peas (climbing) •	
Temperate Climate		
Artichoke shoots	Carrots ••••	Peas (dwarf) •
Asparagus	Lettuce	Potato tubers ••••
Beets ••••	Onions	Rhubarb
Broad beans	Parsnip ••••	Spinach
Cabbage	Peas (climbing) •	Swiss chard ••••
Subtropical climate		
Asparagus	Eggplant	Rhubarb crowns
Beans (climbing)	Lettuce	Scallions
Beans (dwarf)	Marrow	Spinach •••
Beets	Melons	Squash
Broad beans	Parsnip	Sweet corn
Broccoli	Peas (climbing)	Swiss chard
Cabbage	Peas (dwarf)	Tomatoes
Carrots	Potato tubers	Turnips
Cucumber	Radish	

parsnip, spinach, Swiss chard, leek, and peas. In warm to tropical frost-free coastal gardens, you will be able to add most of the summer-growing crops as well. Remember to practice crop rotation and plant them in different beds.

Strawberries are also a good cool season crop. Virus-free plants are available through autumn and winter. Keep the beds well mulched with straw for weed-free beds and clean fruit.

When early-planted broad beans are in full flower, pinch out the growing tips to encourage fruit set. The tips can be cooked lightly and eaten.

Winter

With the exception of the dormant perennials, such as rhubarb and asparagus crowns, which become available in winter, most of the winter vegetable garden should already be planted by the time winter comes around. There are, however, some vegetables that can be planted through winter in most areas. Choose from broad beans, spinach, radish, parsley, onion (mid-season varieties), leek, shallots, artichoke offshoots, winter lettuce varieties, horseradish roots, and peas (where frosts are not likely at flowering time).

In very cold districts, winter plantings are best limited to broad beans, cabbage, and horseradish, while frost-free coastal districts can add cabbage, beets, potato sets, and turnip. In warm coastal sub-tropical to tropical areas, almost anything can go in including what are regarded as summer crops in cooler areas, such as tomato, zucchini, cucumber, celery, peppers, and French beans.

In fact, for the gardener in warm to hot areas, winter is a great time to get vegetables growing. You needn't worry about wet season rains, high humidity which encourages fungal disease or heat, which favors the hordes of sucking and chewing insect pests. It is still important to watch for insect attack, from two-spotted mite and bean fly for instance, and spray when necessary.

Autumn planted crops should be growing well and some will be ready to start picking. Leafy plants such as cabbage, lettuce, Swiss

Preparing for Spring

In late January in coastal areas, start a few tomato seeds in Jiffy pots on a warm windowsill or in a greenhouse if you have one.

Tomato seedlings can be potted on and grown ready to plant out as soon as the weather is warm enough.

If you have room for the Jiffy pots, you ought like to try planting up some other early plants to get the jump on the season. Plant about three seeds to a Jiffy pot and thin to the strongest plant after the first true leaves appear.

If you have a sunny, sheltered porch or patio, the seedlings could be potted when large enough and stay in pots or troughs until ready to go into the garden.

chard and celery, can be given a light side-dressing of sulfate of ammonia or can be watered over with Nitrosol or a similar foliar fertilizer when in mid-growth.

Peas can also be fed now.

If sowing carrots in January, do not enrich the soil with manures as, along with clods or stones in the soil, manures will cause misshapen and forked roots. Prepare the soil well by forking the soil so that it is crumbly.

Protect developing cauliflower curds from direct sunlight, which discolors the white curd and makes it yellowish, by bending the longer, outer leaves over and tying them so that the center of the plant is shaded.

Broad beans will need support—even the dwarf varieties. Put stakes at each end of the row (add an extra one in the middle if rows are long) and run some garden twine along so that plants are held up.

Pest control is still necessary in winter. There will still be a few cabbage butterflies around even in winter, except in very cold areas, so don't forget to protect your brassicas (cabbage, cauliflower, brussels sprouts, kohlrabi, turnip, radish, broccoli). Maintain your checks under the leaves and pick off caterpillars or dust with Derris. Also, watch for aphids that may be around on winter crops, especially cabbage aphids and black aphids on onions. Spray invaders with pyrethrum.

During the cooler weather it is safe

to use white oil and dusting sulfur, which are environmentally friendly controls but have the capacity to burn plants during hot weather. White oil is good for pests, especially scale, and dusting sulfur is a treatment for fungal diseases.

The vegetable garden will need watering in winter but it is important not to water unless the soil is dry. Water when necessary in the morning so that soil has a chance to warm up through the day and the plants will dry off. If you have an overnight frost, get out into the garden as early as possible before the sun shines on the plants and water to melt the frost before it can burn the vegetables.

If you're lucky enough to have alligator lizards or fence lizards in your area, they will control snails without the need to use baits. Lizards that do eat baited snails will in turn be poisoned

Pest and Disease Control

Insect Control

Once your plants are up, check them daily for signs of insect attack. Warnings include holes in leaves, curled leaves, and aphids on new growth. Spend one or two minutes of your time walking between the rows and looking for these signs. As insects tend to hide under the leaves, spot check by running your hands quickly up the plants to expose the undersides. You needn't look under every leaf, but if you do find telltale signs of attack—droppings, chewed leaves, webbing—check more carefully.

One or two aphids signal the presence of many more scattered through the plants. Reach for the insect spray and give plants a quick squirt under the leaves.

The quickest treatment for caterpillars and snails is to remove any you spot and crush them underfoot. If you see the silvery trails but they don't lead to the perpetrator, sprinkle a little snail bait around the base of the plants. Remember that snail bait is poisonous to pets, birds, and children, so use it sparingly and cover it with a large cabbage leaf or something similar so that only the slugs and snails will find it.

If you don't want to use snail bait, try this method of controlling snails. You'll need a length of terracotta agricultural pipe and a tin of pet food. Dampen the pipe and place a spoonful of pet food in its center so that your pets can't reach it. Place the pipe lengthwise in the garden bed. The snails will be attracted to the cool damp pipe as well as to the pet food. Check the pipe each morning. Scrape out the accumulated snails with a stick and squash them or drop them into a bucket of well-salted water. Re-bait and dampen the pipe and put it back

The five-minute vegetable gardener should learn not to panic at the sight of one or two holes chewed in the cabbages and other vegetables. You won't have time to obtain 100 percent perfect plants. Shrug off minor attacks—it is the outer leaves of cabbages and other leafy plants that are usually chewed, and you wouldn't eat those anyway.

Crop Rotation for One Bed for Eighteen Months

In its simplest definition crop rotation means not growing vegetables from the same family in the same place two seasons in a row. The advantages of this very basic idea are that it breaks the breeding and growth cycles of pests and diseases because the conditions change each season.

This alone is a good enough reason to practice crop rotation. But by paying a bit more attention to the needs of different vegetable families, you can take advantage of each vegetable's particular habits to encourage the best possible growth and cropping.

Let's start with legumes, for example. They put lots of nitrogen into the soil, which benefits leaf crops, such as Swiss chard and the brassicas. so it makes sense to put them in after a crop of peas or beans. Follow the leaf crops with tomatoes and other fruiting vegetables and then put in the root crops. Too much nitrogen causes leaf growth at the expense of root growth for plants such as carrots and beets, so putting them in a couple of seasons after the legumes gives them the best chance to develop well. Follow the root crops with a fallow season, leaving the bed manured, composted, and mulched, but empty, or grow a green manure crop. Then it's back to the legumes. This kind of crop rotation practice might look like this. In one bed peas are planted in autumn and harvested in winter. Lettuce and brussels sprouts are planted in winter and harvested in spring, sweet corn and zucchini are planted in spring and harvested in late summer and carrots are planted in autumn and harvested in winter. The bed stays fallow until the next spring planting of beans.

If you're factoring onions into your plan, take account of their love of lime and put them in before the legumes. Follow the legumes with leaf crops, the leaf crops with root crops and the root crops with tomatoes. The soil will gradually become more acidic as the seasons pass so that by the time the acid-loving tomatoes have their turn, the soil will be perfect for them.

Autumn Planting
Peas

Winter Planting
Brussel Sprouts, Lettuce

Spring Planting
Corn, Zucchini

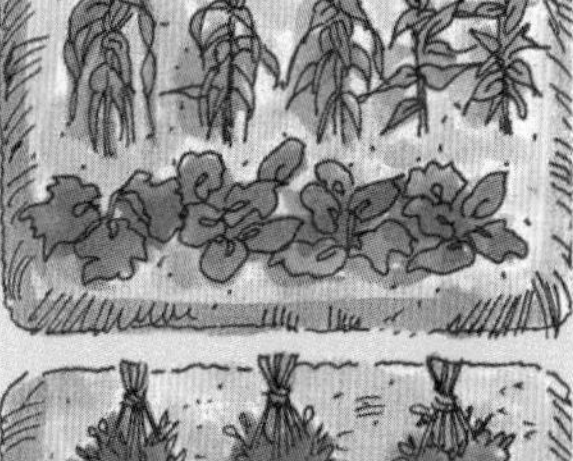

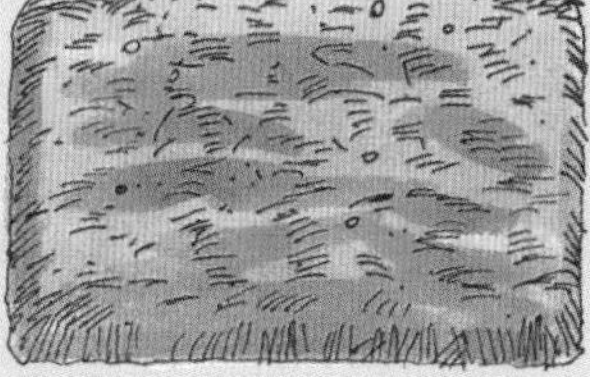

Autumn Planting
Carrots

Winter Planting
Fallow

Spring Planting
Beans

in the garden. This method is totally effective, provided you check the pipe daily and remove the snails.

Members of the cabbage family are best kept dusted with Derris as a precaution against cabbage white butterfly. Interplanting cabbages and other members of the brassica tribe with strong-smelling herbs will help deter cabbage white butterfly. The smell of the herbs masks the smell of the cabbage.

Companion planting is particularly effective in this instance because the cabbage white butterfly smells through its feet and searches for the scent of plants of the cabbage family on which to lay its eggs. Interplanting vegetable crops with herbs is an effective way of deterring other insect predators as well.

Nasturtiums are also often used as companion plants. They repel whitefly and are planted near broccoli to keep the aphids away and around apple trees to repel woolly aphids. If you're nervous about letting nasturtiums loose in your veggie rows, plant them somewhere else in the garden and use the leaves to make a tea. Pour boiling water over the leaves, steep, and when cool use the strained liquid as a spray over your vegetables to repel insects.

The best prevention against insect attack, though, is to keep plants growing steadily and strongly. Healthy plants

The Fruit Fly Circus

Fruit fly can decimate your veggie crop, especially those luscious tomatoes. Female fruit flies lay eggs in any mature or ripening fruit except pineapples, including the fruits of flowering peaches, japonica, crabapple, jujube, and other fruit-bearing ornamental trees and shrubs. You can expect fruit fly to be a real nuisance from June until October. Picking fruit early will lessen the chance of attack, but you will also need a control program and it requires chemicals.

The first step is to hang up a chemical lure. Or you can make your own lure using two empty soft drink bottles and a spoonful of honey, cider vinegar, or ripe bananas. Mix the honey (or banana) with enough water to form a liquid and pour it into one of the bottles. Screw on the lid. Cut the top off the second lid to form a small funnel. Make a hole in the side of the first bottle large enough to screw the cut-off top in to form an entrance. Hang the lure near plants likely to be attacked by fruit fly. They will fly down into the bottle through the funnel but will be unable to get back out again. Check the lure or lures frequently and when you see a build-up of trapped insects, its time to start spraying.

Cover sprays are sprayed over foliage and fruit and kill the tiny larvae after they hatch from eggs laid in the fruit. A chemical used is carbaryl. Don't harvest until at least a week after spraying.

The alternative to cover sprays is to use splash baits. This is splashed with a brush onto foliage, stems, stakes, or nearby fencing, but not on the fruit itself.

Birds

Remember that not all birds are pests. Many native birds feed on nectar but also devour insect pests. Attract desirable birds to the garden by planting a few native flowers near the vegetable bed.

are not as attractive to predators as weak ones. When plants are about half-grown, give a side dressing of blood and bone to maintain steady growth. Leafy crops, such as lettuce and Swiss chard, will respond well to a weekly watering over the leaves with a foliar fertilizer such as Nitrosol. Do this in the cool of the day.

Disease Control

Reduce the possibility of disease by sensible management. Practice simple crop rotation to avoid a build-up of pests or diseases in the soil. This means not growing the same plants, or plants of the same family in the same bed each year and following leaf crops with root crops.

Plant disease-resistant vegetable varieties and keep weeds away from the vegetable garden. Weeds are often hosts to other pests and diseases that move onto vegetables once they are growing well. Stop disease in its tracks by culling any sick plants before the problem can spread. Put diseased plants straight into the garbage bin. Don't leave them lying on the ground and don't put them into your compost bin.

Bird and Animal Control

Birds are often a problem in the vegetable garden and there are several methods of keeping them from eating your crop. A traditional method of keeping birds away from crops is to crisscross the bed with string threaded with pieces of silver foil. The silver foil (some people use bits of the foil from Christmas streamers) flutters, rattles, and flashes in the sun, which makes the birds uneasy and unable to land.

Serious problems with birds and possums might require netting. Stretch it firmly so that birds and other animals don't get tangled and injured. Many commercial orchards are now screened to protect fruit from the depredations of birds and animals and, though costly, it is totally effective. Orchardists have been amazed at how much extra fruit they harvest when the birds and animals don't take a share of the produce.

For rows of low-growing vegetables—cabbage, lettuce, strawberries, Swiss

If you have problems with pets or small children digging up your garden, picking the vegetables, or eating the snail bait (which is poisonous to dogs, cats, birds and small children if they eat enough), put a quick fence right around your garden. The cheapest and quickest way of doing this is to drive a few star pickets around the garden, then wrap a length of plastic mesh fencing around the pickets. This type of fencing isn't the most aesthetically pleasing, but it only takes a couple of minutes to put up and can be taken down and moved as required.

chard, etc.—it is simple to make tunnels of chicken wire or fine plastic mesh over hoops of fencing wire. Made in any convenient length, these are light and easy to move and can be used to cover rows of plants under threat, such as germinating seeds, developing vegetables, and fruiting strawberries.

The five-minute gardener doesn't have time to mess around with ineffectual deterrents, so select the one most likely to be effective in your circumstances.

Cats and dogs (often other people's) can be a problem in the backyard veggie garden. There are many simple folk-methods of persuading pets to stay off the garden. These include sprinkling cayenne pepper, moth balls, or commercial pet repellant around the garden or growing a bush of the herb rue, clipping it and scattering the leaves over newly planted beds. Unfortunately these methods don't always work. A stake and wire netting fence right around the garden is more effective.

Possums are a common problem in both suburban and country gardens. A safe and reliable deterrent is to spread bits of wool straight from the sheep around the garden. Discarded dags are best.

Hang the wool on fences too if possums climb the fence to gain access to the garden.

Gardens troubled by rabbits should be surrounded by a wire netting fence. Bury the netting well down in the soil and bend it outwards so that as the animal digs, it keeps striking the wire.

Gardeners competing for the harvest with these thieves will need to cover the top of the garden with netting, supported by the fence posts. One option is to use lengths of wire netting that can be lifted up like a lid and folded back when you want to work.

In country and even outer-suburban areas, vegetable gardens may need to be protected from grazing stock. An electric fence is easy and practical if the usual fences of stakes and mesh aren't effective.

Control from Nature

Five-minute gardeners need all the help they can get. It makes sense to enlist nature. You've already discovered the time-saving benefits of composting and mulching which cuts down on the time spent watering and weeding. We've discussed the value of interplanting vegetables with strong-smelling herbs to discourage insect pests.

But not all the insects in your garden are pests. There are many friendly insects that feed on aphids, caterpillars, leafhoppers, mealy bugs, and other enemies of the five-minute vegetable gardener. These garden allies include assassin bugs, dragonflies, ladybugs, praying mantis, hoverflies, lacewings, and spiders. Other insects, including small wasps, parasitize the eggs of harmful insects and prevent them from hatching. Bees are garden friends too and pollinate vegetables as they visit flowers collecting pollen and nectar.

Encourage these friendly insects by avoiding the use of harmful chemical sprays whenever possible. Rely instead on organic sprays such as pyrethrum, soap, and Derris, and on sprays made from homegrown herbs such as pennyroyal, wormwood, and bugbane.

Go one step further by inviting these insects into the garden with plants they like. These include herbs such as bergamot, Phacelia, rosemary, and lavender.

Much research in the US and Britain has aimed to determine the extent of the activity of predatory insects and the plants they need for habitat. This research makes for big business—commercial growers buy huge quantities of laboratory-bred predatory insects to help protect their crops from insect pests.

What's Wrong With My Vegetables?

If all is not well in your garden, look for these common pest and diseases. The sooner you identify and treat any problem the smaller that problem will be.

Pests

Aphids

These are small, soft insects that cluster mostly young growth but some, such as cabbage aphids, are also found under the leaves. They may be green, pink, or black. They appear first in early

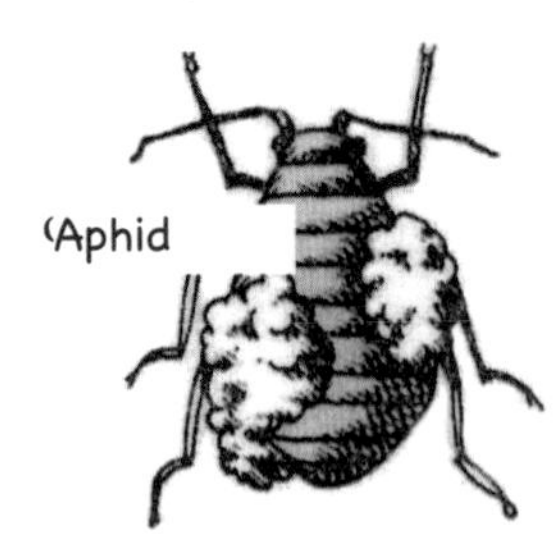
(Aphid

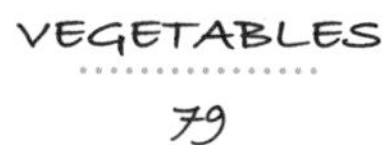

spring with the new growth. Spraying should begin immediately as they multiply fast and cause curling and wilting of foliage; they also spread viral diseases.

Control

Spray with pyrethrum or soap sprays (such as Safer) neither of which will kill predators, such as ladybugs.

Caterpillars

Caterpillars are the larvae of moths and butterflies. The most notorious in the veggie

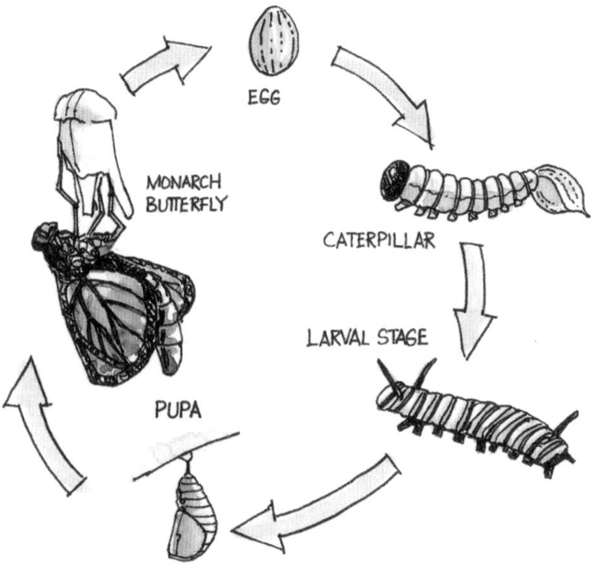

EGG
CATERPILLAR
LARVAL STAGE
PUPA
MONARCH BUTTERFLY

Know Your Caterpillar

One caterpillar every gardener should be able to recognize is the caterpillar of the white cabbage butterfly which is smooth and bright green. Don't spare it or it will destroy all the members of cabbage family in your garden.

Caterpillars are the larvae of moths or butterflies. To save yourself a lot of work, break the life cycle of these pests early. Attacking the larvae stage will give you peace later.

garden is the white cabbage butterfly larvae, which attacks all members of the cabbage family. These are bright green and smooth, growing to 1 inch (30mm). They feed on both sides of the leaves, mostly at night.

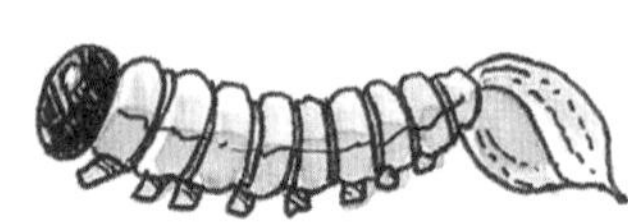
Caterpillar

Control

Dust with Derris or spray with Safer Caterpillar Killer and control weeds. Caterpillars are worse in warm weather.

Cutworm

These pests chew through plant stems near ground-level causing plants to topple over. Young cutworms will also feed on leaves. Several different types do damage at different seasons and following good rains. Cutworm characteristics include: smooth bodies, curling into a flat ball if disturbed, feeding at night and

Cutworms

staying under the surface of the soil by clay, attacking vegetables, seedlings, and strawberries.

Control

Spray with carbaryl over soil and plants in the late afternoon. Try Safer Caterpillar Killer for organic control. To catch them in action, go out after dark with a flashlight.

Fruit Fly

This is the worst pest of fruit and some vegetables. Tomatoes, peppers, eggplants, and most soft fruit are all vulnerable to attack. Cucumber flies also attack all cucurbits, pawpaw, and tomato. Adult fruit fly is small (¼ inch/7mm) with clear wings. The larvae, often called maggots, feed in fruit, causing it to go soft, rot, and fall off the plant.

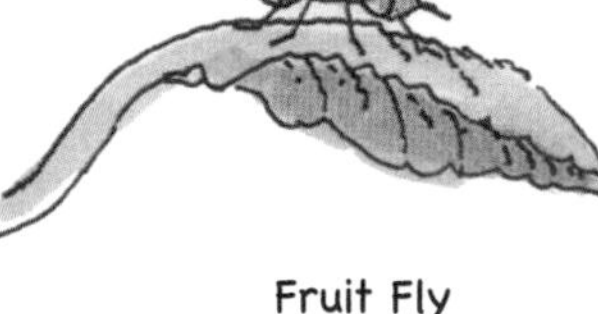

Fruit Fly

Control

Spray early-fruiting plants in the garden, such as loquat and citrus before the flies spread to vegetables. Grow early-maturing crops to miss the worst infestations of late summer. Pick and destroy all infected and fallen fruit (put it in a tightly-tied plastic bag and leave it in the hot sun for a few days, then put it into the garbage bin). Begin spraying when fruit is reaching its mature size, using carbaryl, following directions on container. Commercial splash baits can be used, or you can make your own using ¼ cup (50g) sugar dissolved in a quart (1L) of water mixed with 1½ teaspoons (7mL) maldison. The mixture is splashed liberally with a pat brush onto leaves, steams, trunks, stakes, or nearby fences, but not onto fruit. Repeat every seven days until after harvest. Pick tomatoes when pink and ripen on a sunny windowsill.

Leaf Miner

Leaf miner

The adults of these pests might be wasps, sawflies, or beetles. Eggs are laid on or in leaves and tiny larvae mine the leaves, leaving wavering white trails through the green leaves of many vegetables and ornamentals.

Control

Pick any severely damaged leaves and put them into the bin. Slightly damaged leaves are still edible. If you want to, you can spray with a systemic such as carbaryl. If you do, follow the withholding period.

Metallic Flea Beetle

This is a small (1/10 inch/3mm) pest with a metallic shine and strong hind legs that allow it to hop like a flea. They chew holes in the leaves and buds of fruit and vegetables such as rhubarb, lettuce, potato, and sweet potato.

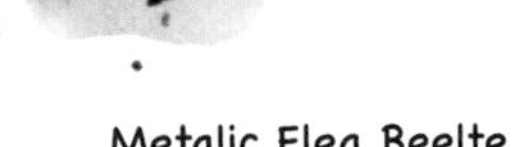
Metalic Flea Beelte

Control

Spray carbaryl as directed in the evening when the bees aren't working.

Mites

There are various mites that damage vegetables and the worst is the two-spotted mite, which is more usually called red spider mite. It attacks beans and other vegetables as well as strawberries, fruit trees, roses, and many ornamentals. Two-spotted mites feed under leaves, leaving reddish nymphal casts and excreta and webbing. Mites can be just seen with the naked eye and are pale-yellowish to green with a dark spot on either side of the body. Damaged leaves become grayish or silvery. Bean leaves have a gray mottling, turn yellow and fall.

Red Spider Mite

Control

Two-spotted mites like dry conditions, so watering over infested plants, making sure to wet under the leaves, may help. Remove and destroy the worst infected leaves, or the whole plant, if it's badly damaged. Control weeds. Predatory mites can be bought and distributed in gardens prone to bad attacks. Alternatively, use dusting sulfur and wettable sulfur (not in hot weather) or spray with carbaryl as directed on the container.

Nematodes

Also called eelworms, these are tiny (invisible to the naked eye) pests found in the roots of vegetables and ornamentals, where they form lumps and knots. Above ground, plants are stunted and yellowish while a mass of fibrous roots forms just below the surface. Tomato nematodes are often a problem, particularly in sandy soils.

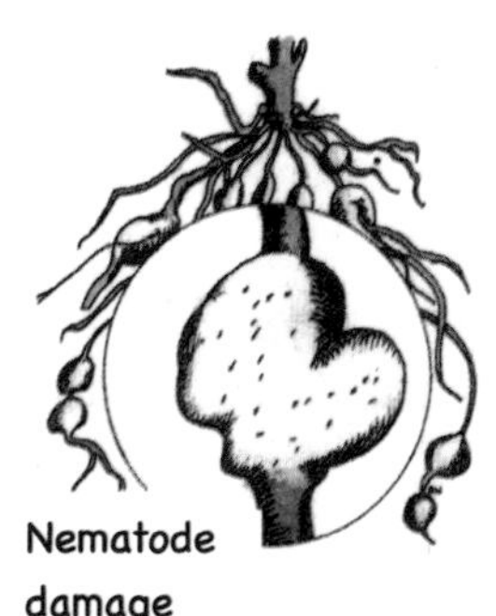
Nematode damage

Control

Remove and destroy damaged plants. Water soil with Nemacur. Plant marigolds (strong-smelling types) for two or three seasons. Do not plant tomatoes in the same areas until you can be sure the nematodes have been eradicated. Observe the principles of crop rotation.

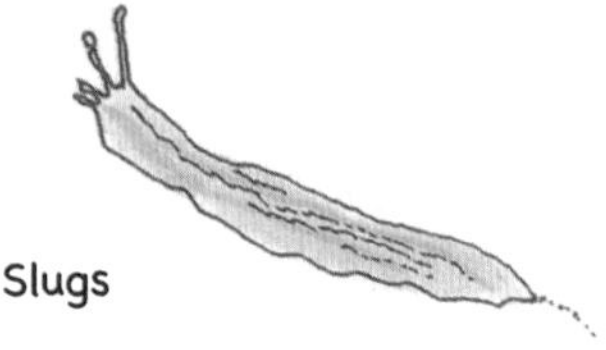
Slugs

Snails and Slugs

Both these chew holes in leaves and buds and can seriously damage seedlings. Snails have a spiral-shaped shell, while slugs don't have a shell at all. They both mainly feed at night and come out thickly on rainy nights or when there is a heavy dew. They congregate in damp places under bricks, pots, etc.

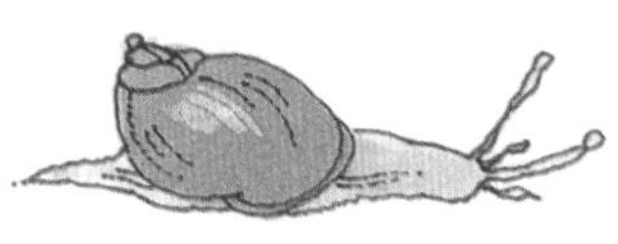
Snail

Control

Put down snail pellets (protect pets by putting pellets in a container). Ducks, such as Indian Runners and Khaki Campbells, will clean up snails and slugs. Handpick snails and slugs at night or early in the morning and drop them into a bucket of salted water.

Thrips

Thrips are always around but are often not noticed unless they are in plague proportions. Thrips are tiny (.06 inches/1.5mm) and are attracted to white and pale-colored flowers and leaves and damage a wide variety of vegetables, including beans (bean blossom thrips), onions (onion thrips), strawberries, and many ornamentals. They are worst in dry weather.

Thrip

Control

Keep infested plants well watered. Heavy rain will often end a plague. Spray with malathion every 10–14 days if necessary.

White Curl Grubs

Whtie Curl Grubs

Larvae of scarab or cockchafer beetles, these are gray, white, or cream with a brown head and characteristically curl into a semicircle when disturbed in the soil by digging. Grubs feed on plant roots, while adults prefer leaves, such as gums, on which they can inflict serious damage. Curl grubs may damage strawberries and other vegetables and are particularly dangerous for potted plants as they can eat almost all the root system.

Control

When you find them throw them onto the lawn for the birds. Water over infested soil with soil insect killer.

Whitefly

With a wingspan of just 1/10 inch (3mm), these look like tiny white moths. They fly up in masses when disturbed and can attack a wide range of vegetables, including beans and tomatoes. Eggs are laid under leaves where the flies multiply quickly in warm weather. This is a serious pest in the greenhouse.

White fly

Control

Spray with whitefly killer and follow withholding period recommendations on fruit and veggies. An effective biological control is to paint pieces of wood with bright yellow paint and smear them liberally with clear grease. Place the boards among the vegetables and the whitefly will fly to them and stick to the grease. Wipe the boards clean during heavy infestations as trapped insects will obscure the yellow color that will attract more willing victims.

Diseases

Anthracnose

This is a fungal disease that attacks many vegetables, including beans, cucumber, lettuce and tomato, as well as other garden plants, including avocado, mango, and rose. Dark brown spots and marks appear on leaves, stems, pods, and fruit. Seed becomes infected. Veins blacken and spots develop into black, sunken craters. Ripening tomato fruit develops ½ inch (12mm) depressions with concentric rings.

Anthrocuose

Control

Practice crop rotation, do not grow plants from infected seed and plant resistant varieties where possible. Spray with Bravo, making sure to wet both sides of the leaves.

Blossom-End Rot

Recognize this problem by brown sunken areas on the blossom end of tomatoes and peppers. Symptoms appear when fruit is half-grown. It is caused by lack of calcium and is worse if the water supply fluctuates.

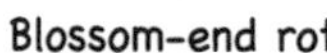

Blossom-end rot

Control

Lime soil or add superphosphate to the soil before planting seedlings. Prevent water-logging of plants and water plants regularly. Treating soil with a surfactant will improve the water-holding ability of the soil. Protect plants from hot, dry winds.

Club Root of Crucifers

This fungal disease causes abnormal development of roots. They are thick in the middle and taper to each end. Infected plants grow slowly and wilt rapidly on hot days. The disease is caused by infected seedlings or contaminated soil—spores can remain in the soil for a long time.

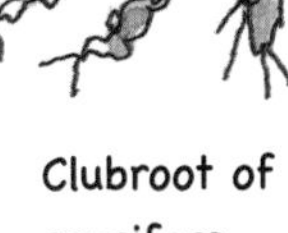

Clubroot of crucifers

Control

Practice crop rotation. Fungal diseases do best in acid soils, so liming the soil will help kill spores. Grow resistant varieties when available.

Damping Off

This fungal disease causes seedlings to topple over suddenly. Seed can be infected and germinating shoots may rot before they appear above the soil. Any seeds or seedlings can be attacked.

Damping off

Control

Water soil before planting seeds with Captan to protect from damping-off fungus. Captan treatment may save seedlings if applied as soon as infection is noticed. Do not overwater them. Discard infected seedlings and soil into garbage bin.

Fungal Spots

Aside from the anthracnose fungal spots, there are a number of other fungal spotting diseases. These include rust, blight, and gray mold that all cause spots on leaves, stems, and fruit of vegetables. Many fungal diseases live in the soil and are carried onto plants by splashing from watering or rain. If fungi are not controlled, leaves rot and fall, and stems and fruit rot.

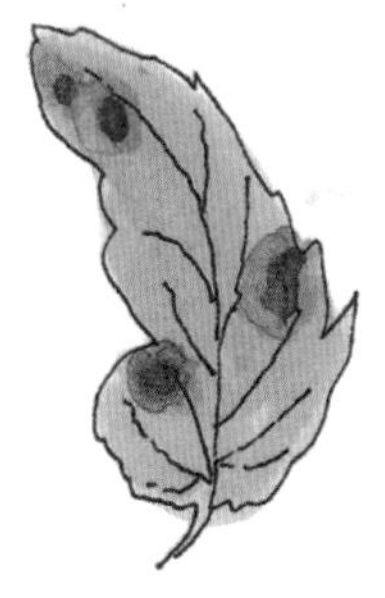

Fungal Spots

Control

Crop rotation is important. Mulching with straw or leaf mulch will prevent fungal spores splashing up from soil.

When plants show sign of disease, pick off and destroy badly infected leaves and spray with a fungicide, such as mancozeb.

Downy Mildew

Downy mildew first appears as light yellow patches spreading between the veins on the top of leaves. These go brown, and white and furry patches appear on the underside of the leaves, and often on the outer leaves of infected lettuce, rhubarb, onion, and peas.

Control

Good air circulation is important; do not grow plants too close together. Do not water over leaves late in the day, and pick off unwanted outer leaves of lettuce that show any symptoms. Spray with Bravo.

Downy mildew

Powdery Mildew

This appears as a white powdery film over the leaf surface and is worst in warm, dry conditions. White spots appear under older leaves, spreading to the leaf surface to form the typical white powdery growth. This disease is common to all members of the cucurbit family (pumpkin, cucumber, squash, watermelon, etc.) and also infects strawberries, pawpaw, and ornamentals. If untreated, leaves brown and shrivel, exposing fruit to sun scald.

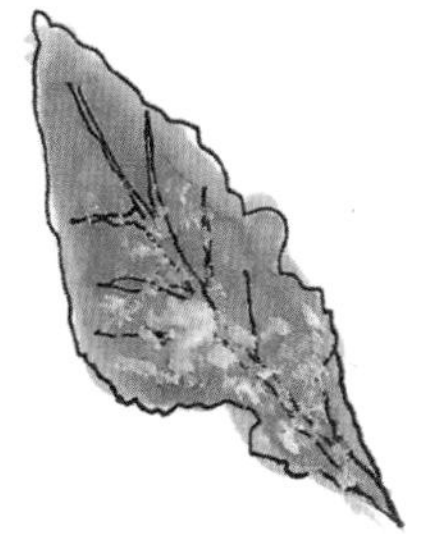
Powdery mildew

Control

Plant mildew-resistant varieties wherever possible. Remove diseased leaves. Spray with potassium bicarbonate, sulfur, or lime sulfur. Treat other infected plants in the garden to remove the pool of mildew spores.

Potato Scab

Also called common scab, this disease begins as brown dots on the skin of potates that increase in size as tubers grow and become corky or pitted so that they may cover most of the surface. The disease is usually not noticed until the potatoes are harvested. It can be introduced into the soil by planting infected tubers and is worst in dry, alkaline soils.

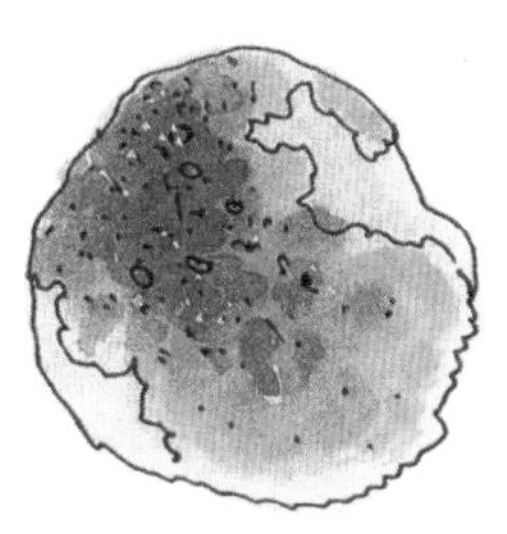
Potato Scab

Control

It is important that disease-free tubers are planted. Avoid liming the soil where the disease is a problem. Water regularly so that tubers are not short of moisture during development. Rotate crops so that potato, turnip, and beet are not planted in the same bed for the next two or three seasons.

Summer Death of Beans

This virus-like disease causes the sudden death or yellowing of beans during hot weather. Plants are stunted and wilted with leaves curled under. Test for the disease by cutting through the lower stem. Discoloration, which progresses to black when the roots rot, indicates disease. It is spread by the brown leafhopper that feeds on infected weeds before attacking beans.

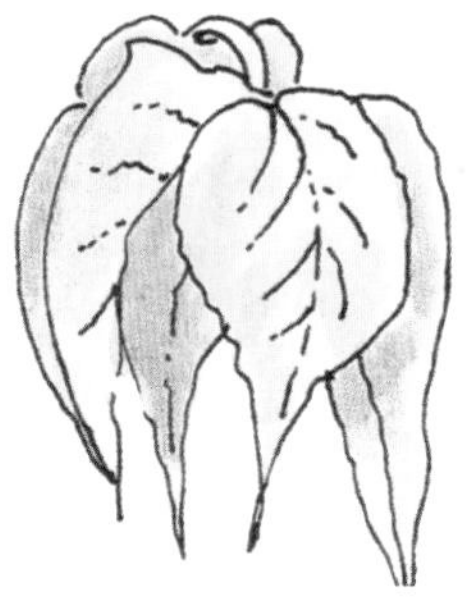

Summer Death of Beans

Control

Keep weeds down to reduce insect populations.
Spray growing plants regularly to control the sucking and chewing insects that spread disease.

Tomato Mosaic

This viral disease causes mottling on the leaves, streaking on stems and sunken brown patches under the skin of fruit. It is spread during handling, pruning, and general gardening by smokers.

Control

Cigarette and pipe tobacco contains this virus and people should not smoke while working in the vegetable garden. Smokers should wash before handling plants.

Tomato Mosaic

Vegetable Selections

Vegetable Selections

Artichoke *

The globe artichoke is a large, handsome perennial that takes up a lot of space; so it probably won't be the first choice of the five-minute vegetable gardener. If you love the exotic flower buds, though, and find room for a couple of plants, artichoke is as easy to grow as a thistle. It prefers a climate where summers are not too hot and winters not too frosty. Seed, if available, can be sown in spring, but shoots are more reliable—beg a couple from an artichoke-growing friend. Shoots should be about 12 inches (30cm) long, with some good roots. Plant them in late winter, or in autumn in areas with mild winters, into well-composted holes 3–5 feet (1–1.5m) apart. Buds appear in early spring and continue until November. Plants should be mulched and watered until autumn, when they are cut back to a height of 12 inches (30cm). After cutting them back give them a dressing of complete fertilizer and a mulch of manure or compost and then in winter prune them back to four or five strong shoots.

Tip: If there is no space in the veggie garden, plant these handsome perennials in the flower garden where they make great accent plants. After three years start renewing the plants by using shoots taken from the original plants, which can then be discarded.

Asparagus *

Asparagus is a perennial that prefers a cool to cold climate and could grow in the garden for the next hundred years—so give it a permanent bed. Asparagus is great for the five-minute vegetable gardener as, once planted, it requires very little attention for long periods of the year. Buy two-year-old crowns in winter. Plant them in a trench dug to spade depth in soil containing generous quantities of compost and other humus and dressed with complete plant food. Set crowns 12–20 inches (30–50cm) apart at the bottom of the trench and cover with an inch (3cm) of soil. Gradually fill in the trench as the ferns grow, taking care not to cover the new shoots. Do not cut any spears in the first spring but allow the plants to grow on, watering and feeding through summer. Cut asparagus down to ground level in winters. Harvesting can begin in the next season, from February or March, and cutting is done every day or so for eight to ten weeks. Once again allow plants to grow strongly through summer with regular feeding and watering and cut down to ground level in winter.

Tip: Asparagus plants are male or female. Male plants give the best spears, so cull the female plants when they set berries in the second autumn.

Beans *

Dwarf or climbing beans give a great yield for space and can be grown year-round in warm, frost-free areas and right through the warm weather in temperate climates. Beans are so easy to grow that they are the number one vegetable choice for home gardeners. Dwarf beans are ready to pick in 8–10 weeks, so make successive sowings by sowing new seed as soon as the previous sowing develops its first true leaves. This way cropping will continue into early autumn. Beans are frost-tender and prefer a bed sheltered from strong winds. Feed with blood and bone or fowl manure and keep rows mulched well to protect the shallow root system. Grow climbing beans on a sunny fence, trellis, or tripod. Make a quick trellis by pushing bamboo stakes into the soil at an angle so that the canes are criss-crossed.

Tip: Beans do well if they follow a crop of heavy feeders such as cabbage or potato which required the ground to be well fertilized.

Broad Beans *

An excellent crop for mild to cool climates, broad beans are planted from autumn to winter. They need support as even the dwarf varieties will grow to 3 feet (1m). Plant in rows with a band of complete fertilizer run alongside. Water the soil the night before so that it is damp-dark when planting. Dust seed with a fungicide before planting an inch (3cm) deep and 6–8 inches (15–20cm) apart. Extra fertilizer should not be needed as the crop grows. Pick young to slice and eat like French beans or leave them to mature. When mature, pods are shelled. For a fancy vegetable dish parboil mature pods then pop the outer skin off to reveal the bright green, tender, delicate flavored inner pod. Toss in butter and finely chopped sage over a low heat.

Tip: Flower-drop in early spring is caused by low temperatures. The problem will be solved when the weather warms up and there are also more bees around to pollinate the flowers.

Beets *

Beets suit rich, loamy soil well-prepared and fed for a previous crop. Don't add fresh manure. In warm to tropical zones sow seed most of the year, avoiding the wet season. Sow January to September in temperate areas and March to August in cold zones. Sow ½ inch (12mm) deep and cover seeds with vermiculite, then mulch bed lightly with dry grass clippings. Thin seedlings to allow roots room to develop. Plants come up in clusters. The roots develop slightly above soil level, so don't cover with mulch or soil. Grow beets quickly by using liquid feeds. Start pulling plants 10 weeks after sowing. Make successive plantings every 4 to 6 weeks for a constant supply.

Tip: When harvesting, pull alternate roots to allow others to grow larger. Beets are excellent served as a hot vegetable as well as the usual pickled salad.

Broccoli **

Broccoli is a good cool climate vegetable and suits any area with some cold winter weather. Sow seed from early summer in cool districts and late summer in warmer areas into slightly alkaline soil well prepared with old manures and a dressing of complete fertilizer. Grow quickly with liquid feeds. When plants develop a central head, cut and use, as this will encourage more growth and side heads. Like the others in the brassica family (brussels sprouts, cabbage, cauliflower, kohlrabi) cabbage white butterfly is a real pest, especially in warm conditions. Control with Derris Dust, or try a companion planting of strong smelling herbs such as sage. Protect from snails and slugs with a ring of sawdust or rice hulls around plants.

Tip: When cutting the central head, cut the stem 4 inches (10cm) on a slant to prevent water lying on cut section causing stem rot. In acid soil, give a light dressing of lime before planting.

Brussels Sprouts **

Brussels sprouts are a good cool season crop not suited to warm climates. Sow seed from April to early August in cold districts and June to late August in temperate areas into soil prepared with old manures and a dressing of complete fertilizer. Transplant seedlings at 24-inch (60cm) spacings and water well. Give regular feeds using liquid fertilizers or blood and bone. Guard against cabbage white butterfly caterpillars with regular sprinklings of Derris Dust and keep snails and slugs away with a physical barrier, such as a ring of sawdust around plants.

Tip: Pick brussels sprouts from the base of the plant up, by cutting or twisting them off. You can expect to start harvesting about 90 days after transplanting. As you pick remove the yellowing lower leaves. Don't attempt this veggie in hot climates.

Cabbage *

Cabbages are best in cool weather but are very adaptable. Plant out from seedlings or sow seed into soil well prepared with lots of old manure and a dressing of complete fertilizer. Stagger plantings so that the whole crop doesn't mature at once (unless you especially like pickled cabbage!) Space at 30 inches (75cm) and keep watered and fed. Use Derris Dust to control cabbage white butterfly caterpillars.

Tip: In summer try Chinese cabbage (pak choy) for quick crops and tender coleslaw or stir-fry. Superette is a good choice for the home garden because it is resistant to bolting and can be picked young or left to mature.

Cauliflower ***

Cauliflower is a slow-growing (14 to 24 weeks) winter vegetable that prefers a cool climate. This doesn't make it a popular crop for the five-minute vegetable gardener. Enthusiasts should grow it from seed sown in pots from July, or from bought seedlings spaced at 20–30 inches (50–75cm), depending on variety. Prepare the bed with old manures and a dressing of complete fertilizer. Dust regularly for caterpillars and check for aphids.

Tip: Blanch curds, if desired, when heads are fist-sized. Gather surrounding leaves together to enclose the head and hold them in position with a rubber band. Check under the leaves regularly for pests and disease. In small spaces grow mini-cauliflowers, such as Garant, which can be sown 6 inches (15cm) apart.

Carrots *

Carrots need deep sandy or loam soils; lumps or stones will cause the carrots to fork. If growing carrots in clay soils, raise the level of the bed with organic matter and sand and grow short stump-rooted varieties. Sow seed from January to September in temperate areas, February to August in cold districts and year-round, except in the hottest months, in warm zones. Before sowing, sprinkle a little complete fertilizer in a band at the base of the furrow and cover with a layer of soil. Sow direct into beds and cover with vermiculite or seed raising mix and water gently. Thin and weed as seedlings grow, until there's 2 inches (5cm) between them. As they grow, mulch lightly to stop the soil from drying out and to keep the roots cool in summer. If growth is slow, stimulate with a liquid fertilizer.

Tip: Don't neglect thinning as roots will grow tangled together if grown too close. Sow carrots and leeks together (more carrots than leeks) for mutual protection from pests.

Celery **

A good choice for the five-minute gardener, celery can be harvested every two or three months by taking stems from the outside of the plant, one at a time. Celery does well in mild and cool areas but is readily grown in warmer areas in late summer and autumn. Raise seedlings in small pots. At 8 to 10 weeks, they are ready to plant out into beds prepared with plenty of manure and a dressing of complete fertilizer. Space plants 12 inches (30cm) apart. To keep celery tender and growing fast, give liquid feeds every two weeks. Spray leaf spot with fungicide if necessary. To blanch, wrap plants in corrugated cardboard or several thicknesses of newspaper loosely tied, or slip a cardboard milk carton over plants three to four weeks before harvesting.

Chayote *

Chayote is rampant and prolific. It is the easiest vine to grow for privacy and shelter in all but cold, frosty climates. Chayote is a perennial and will grow for years. Sprout the fruit indoors in late winter or early spring, then plant it where it can climb on a fence or trellis. Chayote isn't fussy about conditions, but prefers soil prepared with plenty of humus and a dressing of complete fertilizer. Plant with the shoot and the top of the fruit just above soil level. Feed every six weeks with a side dressing of complete fertilizer. Pick fruit young, about 2 inches (5cm) long, when it is tender and has a delicate flavor.

Tip: Use chayote vines to shade the fowl house and keep hens cool in summer.

Cucumber *

Grow cucumbers in ground well prepared with compost, manure, and a dressing of complete fertilizer. Cucumbers are space-saving grown up a trellis, along a fence or among sweet corn, where it will scramble up the stems. Sow seed direct in warm weather, in pots if cool. Dust seed with fungicide before planting and sow four or five seeds in clumps 18 inches (45cm) apart. Make a slight depression around each clump so that water runs to the roots. Thin to the two strongest plants in each clump. Do not water from above as cucumbers are liable to develop mildew if leaves remain damp. Water well throughout the growing season and give side dressings of blood and bone when flowering stars.

Tip: Brow mildew-resistant varieties such as Burpless to avoid mildew problems. No apple cucumber varieties are resistant to mildew.

Eggplant *

A warm-climate plant belonging to the potato family, eggplant requires at least four months of warm weather. Plant it from March to September in tropical and subtropical areas. In temperate zones, stop planting after June in cold districts, plant only from April to May. Space plants 24–30 inches (60–75cm) apart as they will grow to 24 inches (60cm) or more and may require staking. Feed through the growing season with a complete fertilizer and mulch the root area through summer.

Tip: Eggplants suffer from the same pests and diseases as tomatoes and peppers and need similar care. Do not grow eggplant where any other member of the potato family was grown the previous season.

Herbs *

Herbs should be grown freely by the five-minute vegetable gardener to encourage bees and predatory insects and to deter pests. Herbs are good companion plants as well as delicious and vitamin-rich additives to food. All need good drainage and sun, though mint and coriander will thrive in part-sun. Herbs don't need much feeding—they are better grown a little bit hard. Mint and basil, though, need regular watering.

Tip: Herbs are great in containers. Find a sunny spot for a window box, hanging basket, or pot.

Leeks *

Leeks can be grown from seed which is transplanted out when 8 inches (20cm) high. The five-minute vegetable gardener, though, will appreciate the convenience of nursery-bought seedlings. Plant in a sunny, well-drained bed well prepared with plenty of compost and old manure. Plant from spring to autumn in temperate and cool areas, late summer/autumn in warm and tropical zones. Seedlings should be 6–8 inches (15–20cm) apart, in a trench 8 inches (20cm) deep. Gradually fill in the trench as the plants grow. Keep watered and feed with a liquid fertilizer every two weeks. Make successive sowings at four-weekly intervals to prolong harvest. Start eating your leeks when the stems are about an inch (2cm) thick—about 12 weeks after transplant.

Tip: Leeks can be blanched when almost fully grown by tying newspaper around them or by sliding an opened cardboard milk carton over the plant.

Lettuce *

Lettuce grows best in well-drained, friable soil with regular watering and feeding. It is important to grow the right varieties for the season and to make successive sowings at three to four-weekly intervals to keep up a regular supply. Sow seed directly where lettuces are to grow. Avoid sowing in very hot weather and keep soil moist until seedlings appear. Protect from snails with baits or with barriers of rice hulls or sawdust and give regular liquids feeds. Non-heartening lettuce, such as mignonette, is suitable for containers and small spaces. In summer do not water lettuce from above in the heat of the day.

Tip: Five-minute vegetable gardeners will appreciate mixed pots of seedlings. Look for Lettuce Combo from BPA and Yates' Combo Lettuce. Mixed seed packets are also available.

Melons *

Rockmelons and watermelons are fruit, but belong to the cucumber family and are popular with veggie gardeners. Give them similar treatment to cucumbers. They need four or five months to reach maturity. For Christmas eating, sow direct in spring when soil has warmed. Prepare the bed with compost and a slow-release fertilizer. In cooler areas start seed in Jiffy pots kept in a warm, sheltered place and plant out when the weather is warm enough. Avoid watering over the leaves to discourage mildew and mulch well around the root area before growth spreads. Pinch out runners when they're 24 inches (60cm) long to induce flowering. As fruit matures protect it from fruit fly with a spraying program.

Tip: Melons are ready to cut when the skin in contact with the soil turns yellow and the melon gives a hollow sound when tapped. Rockmelons are ripe when the stem comes away readily.

Onion **

There are early, mid-season and late onions and it is important to plant the right variety for the season. Save time by planting seedlings, as onions take up to seven months to grow from seed. Prepare the soil well and fertilize before planting. Weed regularly and don't mulch because bulbs form just above the surface and need good air circulation. Onions are ready when tops dry and topple over. Pull and leave to dry off in the sun for a few days before storing inside.

Tip: Grow scallions or shallots from spring through autumn for a quick harvest (8 to 12 weeks). Scallions are also ideal for garden edging or containers. Use them to flavor salads or in cooked dishes which benefit from a mild onion flavor.

Oriental vegetables *

Oriental vegetables are ideal for the five-minute vegetable gardener and are just as good for the five-minute cook. There is a wide variety available in seed packets. All grow fast and taste great in stir-fries, salads, and soups.

Tip: Great for small gardens.

Parsnip ***

Parsnips need deep, friable soil and good drainage for good root growth. Plant them in a bed that was well-fertilized for a previous crop, or prepare a bed a month before planting by digging in compost, rotted manure and a dressing of complete fertilizer to spade depth. Parsnip is a good winter crop and grows in all climates, taking about four or five months to mature. In temperate areas sow seed from January to September, in cold climates sow seed from February to August and in tropical and warm climates sow seed August to March. Care for parsnips as you would for carrots.

Tip: Parsnips are notoriously hard to germinate. Seed must be fresh and the soil must not be allowed to dry out at germination time. For best results, water the bed then sow directly into rows, covering the seed with a thin layer of vermiculite. Keep the seedbed covered with damp burlap or newspaper until the first shoots appear.

Peas *

Peas are a good cool-season crop and yield well for space, especially if you grow a climbing pea, such as Telephone, on a 6½-foot (2m) trellis. Dwarf or semi-dwarf peas will need some support—usually from sticks pushed firmly into the soil and criss-crossed to form a tripod. A light dressing of lime should be applied two or three weeks before planting and raked and watered in. When sowing, run a dressing of complete fertilizer along the furrow beside where the peas are to be planted. Cover so that the peas do not come into direct contact with the fertilizer. Dust peas with a fungicide and sow into soil that is damp-dark. This will mean that the peas will not need watering until they have germinated. As the plants grow, mulch them to protect the roots and suppress weeds. Water carefully below the foliage to prevent mildew. When plants flower, give them a side dressing of liquid manure.

Tip: Do not plant peas when there is a risk of frost at flowering time, which occurs about six weeks after sowing.

Pepper *

Bell peppers are sweet and mild, chili peppers are small and hot. Both do best in warm climates where night temperatures don't drop too much and you can count on four months of settle weather. Give both plenty of organic matter and regular watering. One chili plant is enough for most families unless you're particularly keen on Asian or Mexican cooking. Tall-growing bell peppers need a stake for support and should be spaced 24–30 inches (60–70cm) apart. When plants start flowering give side dressings of complete fertilizer and water in.

Tip: Peppers make handsome pot plants but must be kept well-watered. Peppers belong to the same family as tomato and eggplant so can be planted at the same time, require similar conditions, and suffer the same pests and diseases.

Potato **

Grow potatoes in good sandy loam through warm weather when frosts are unlikely. In tropical areas avoid planting through the wet season. Plant virus-free seed potatoes. If these are not available in your area, use healthy, firm, small potatoes. Allow potatoes to green in a shady but brightly lit spot before planting. Dig over the soil to spade depth and add plenty of well-rotted manure and compost. Mark out furrows 6 inches (15cm) deep and run a dressing of complete fertilizer (1/12 cup per foot, 1/4 cup per meter) along the row, covering it with about 2 inches (5cm) soil. Place tubers along furrows 12–16 inches (30–40cm) apart and cover with soil. As plants grow hill up the rows to protect the potatoes from light and potato moth. Potatoes are ready to harvest when the foliage begins to yellow.

Tip: Keeping potatoes well-mulched with a thick layer of straw, hay, or leaf mulch between the rows will increase the crop and protect it from the sun—"green" potatoes are poisonous.

Pumpkin *

Pumpkin is a good choice for the five-minute gardener. The plants need space but have a long growing season and more or less take care of themselves. In small gardens, plant bush pumpkins. Plant all pumpkins in spring (and summer in the tropics) in beds previously prepared with complete fertilizer, manure, and compost. Four to six seeds are planted in raised hills or stations, 4 inches (10cm) apart. Side dressings of liquid manure can be given when the fruit has begun growing. Whenever possible water early in the morning, taking care not to wet foliage. This will discourage mildew. Pumpkin is mature when the vines begin to die down, but the fruit can be picked as soon as the skin is hard. Cut the fruit with a short stem to prevent it from rotting.

Tip: If fruit is not setting, hand-pollinate by brushing pollen from male flowers onto female flowers. You'll identify the female flower by the swollen ovary at the base of the flower. Hand-pollinating is best done in the morning when flowers are fresh and the pollen is least likely to have been affected by sun or wind.

Radish *

Another member of the cabbage family, radish is quick and easy to grow. It's ready to eat just four weeks after sowing. Radishes may be round, oval, long, white, or red. Japanese long white radish (daikon) is used in stir-fry and is sown in late summer for a winter harvest. Sow radish seed thinly in shallow drills and make repeat sowings every two or three weeks. Keep plants watered and give liquid feeds for fast, even growth. Pick radishes when they're young, crisp, and delicately flavored.

Tip: Ideal for children or beginner gardeners, radishes work well in window boxes or containers.

Rhubarb *

Rhubarb is not really a veggie but is still a popular crop for the home vegetable gardener. It's a perennial that forms a good clump and crops well for several years. Rhubarb is planted from crowns available in winter, or from small pots that are sometimes available in spring. It suits most soils with good drainage and added manure and compost. Plants will grow in full sun or part-shade and should be given a dressing of compost or manure each winter to stimulate spring growth. Pick outside leaves as they are needed and give occasional feeds of liquid fertilizer through the growing season. Keep plants well-mulched with compost and manure and well-watered through summer. Three-year-old clumps can be divided in winter.

Tip: The stalk is the edible part of rhubarb and should be cooked in glass or enamel containers as aluminum reacts with the oxalic acid in the rhubarb to make it taste very bitter. The leaves are poisonous and can be used as a potent insect spray for sucking and chewing insects. Simply boil up the leaves, strain the liquid, and dilute it with water before using.

Spinach *

True spinach is a cool season crop that suits cooler areas, where it can be sown from late summer though winter to spring. Grow spinach in the same way as lettuce, with plenty of compost added to well-drained soil. Keep mulched, water, and feed with liquid fertilizer. Pick outside leaves and plants will keep producing for about a month. Watch out for the leaf miner that leaves white tracks through leaves. Pull off affected leaves and eat them, white tracks and all, or cut off the affected part of the leaf and eat the rest.

Tip: Don't bother trying to grow spinach in warm climates.

Squash *

Grow the tender little button squash as you would cucumber, planting them as early as possible in the spring to avoid the pests that are a problem later in the growing season. Grow them in ground well-prepared with compost, manure, and complete fertilizer. Dust seed with fungicide before planting and sow them in stations 18 inches (45cm) apart, four or five seeds per station. Once they start growing, thin them to the strongest two seedlings. Water well through the growing season, taking care not to wet foliage and keep them growing well with side dressings of blood and bone when flowering starts. Regular picking of the bite-sized fruit encourages further fruiting.

Tip: In small gardens try growing squash in containers.

Strawberry *

Though a fruit, strawberry is a great plant for the five-minute vegetable gardener. Grow only certified virus-free plants, which are available in nurseries in autumn and winter. In cool and mild districts Alpine strawberries grown from seed are excellent. Grow strawberries in well-drained soil with plenty of compost dug in, as a border around the vegetable garden, or in rows. As a time-saver with weeding and watering, the rows can be watered well then covered with strips of black polythene held down at the sides with soil. Plant through slits in the plastic. Add a straw mulch when fruiting starts to prevent fruit rotting on the ground.

Tip: Birds, slugs, and snails are all threats to strawberries. Stretch netting over plants and keep up the snail bait as soon as berries start to appear.

Sweet Corn *

Sweet corn needs three to five months of warm weather and grows well in most well-drained soils, given the addition of compost and complete fertilizer. Sow in spring directly into damp-dark soil in blocks of short rows so that plants are clustered together. This aids pollination. Run a band of fertilizer along the furrows and cover before planting seed 6 inches (15cm) apart. Make sure seed doesn't come into contact with the fertilizer. Cover lightly with a layer of mulch to keep soil damp. Aim at about 24 plants after thinning to 10 inches (25cm) apart and make a further sowing when plants are 6 inches (15cm) high. Give side dressings of high nitrogen fertilizer as plants grow and again as soon as tassels begin to appear. Water thoroughly twice a week and keep plants weeded and hilled up around stems. Pick cobs when silk turns brown.

Tip: Overhead watering in the early morning when tassels are ready to shed pollen will promote good pollination. Pollen is shed around midmorning for several days.

Swiss Chard *

A very popular home-grown veggie, Swiss chard can be grown in all areas, year-round in warm climates. Swiss chard is best sown direct as transplanting slows growth. Before sowing, sprinkle fertilizer in a band below the planting furrow and cover with soil. Sow seed and cover with ½ inch (12mm) of vermiculite then water gently. Pick leaves as needed from the outside of the plant. Keep Swiss chard growing quickly with side dressings of liquid fertilizers.

Tip: Before planting soak seed overnight then dust with fungicide. Late autumn sowings may bolt (run to seed).

Tomato **

A must for summer salads, tomatoes can be planted year-round in warm and tropical areas. In temperate areas, start early fruit in Jiffy pots on a windowsill or in a greenhouse in late January, ready to plant out as soon as the soil warms. Otherwise plant seedlings of grafted plants in March. Be generous with manure, compost, and complete fertilizer dug in before planting. Water well. Tall tomatoes will need two-meter stakes put in at planting time. Non-staking varieties, such as Egg tomato, or Early Crop, are easier to grow but need wider spacing 30–39 inches (75–100cm) apart. Dwarf tomatoes such as Patio Hybrid and Tiny Tim are ideal for containers. Most tomatoes will require more attention from the five-minute gardener than other vegetables, including the control of fruit fly though a spraying program. Five-minute gardeners might opt for the easy option of the tiny “wild” tomatoes which come up freely from seed saved, are not troubled by diseases or pests and need little care.

Tip: Do not grow tomatoes in the same bed each year. Destroy plants with wilt, which may be caused by a virus, bacteria, or root nematode.

Turnip *

Turnips and swedes are members of the cabbage family and are good winter crops. They are easily grown in a bed that was well-manured for a previous crop, such as tomatoes. Plant in late summer and autumn, and in cold areas sow also in later winter and early spring. Sow seed where turnips are to grow and keep water until seeds germinate a few days later. Turnips (white flesh) grow more quickly than swedes (yellow flesh) and are best grown fast and eaten when young and fresh. Give side dressings of liquid manure while growing. The bulbous root (swollen stem) sits on the soil surface. Guard against cabbage-loving caterpillars with Derris Dust.

Tip: Swedes are a long-keeping, useful soup and stew vegetable. Try modern varieties for a new approach to the turnip.

Zucchini *

One of the easiest members of the cucumber family to grow, zucchini is deservedly popular with the home gardener. Grow from seedlings for quickest results. Plant when the weather warms in spring, with 20 inches (50cm) space all around the seedlings. Keep watered, watering under the leaves to avoid mildew. A weekly feed of liquid fertilizer will keep plants growing quickly. Frequent picking will encourage more flowering and fruiting.

Tip: Bush zucchinis will suit containers. Pick zucchini small with the flower still attached and stir-fry in olive oil.

One does not begin to make
a garden until he wants a garden.
To want a garden is to be interested
in plants, in the winds and rains,
in birds and insects, in the
warm-smelling earth.

~Liberty Hyde Bailey

chapter 4

Flowers

Ideas for a Five-Minute Flower Garden

The Right Place

The five-minute flower gardener will be able to dream about a whole garden brimming with flowers, each border overflowing with blooms, baskets of color cascading from every beam and brilliant island beds sunning themselves in perfect lawns. But the five-minute gardener needs to recognize such an image as entirely unattainable without a team of full-time workers who might be supervised in just five minutes a day.

Instead the five-minute gardener will focus time and attention on just one area. Restraining your plantings to a single area, instead of trying to fill every space, will mean your plants can be tended easily and quickly. The key to success for the five-minute gardener is good planning and efficient work methods.

Your flowers can be in a special bed made for the purpose. Such a bed might be heart or diamond-shaped and positioned on one side of the front path as was all the rage in Victorian times. Your flower bed might just as well be border plantings on either side of the garden path, a changing pattern of annuals anchored by a couple of standard roses. The fronts of established beds might be taken over for flowers, with existing permanent plants, such as roses, acting as a backdrop.

Many flowers are just as keen about sunshine as a lawn. If you're tiring of mowing, why not give over some of the green to a tapestry of floral color. An organic shape might gently wind its way around, with lawn still encircling it. You might favor a more formal approach, with a circle centered by a birdbath or sundial, in the manner of an old-fashioned herb garden.

Paved areas are a perfect place to practice the skills of the five-minute gardener. Annuals give a bright display grown in a variety of containers (pots, troughs, hanging baskets, window boxes) and add individuality and interest to balconies and courtyards.

Rockeries, particularly new ones, are ideal for growing flowering annuals—they romp away in the sun and warmth, taking your new rock garden from bare to beautiful very quickly. A planting of annuals in the rockery will also fill the space, repressing weeds until the slower-growing rockery plants become established.

Wherever you decide to concentrate on flowers, take some time to consider the conditions of the patch, noting hours of sunlight and soil type, so that you make the right choices of plants. The five-minute gardener doesn't want to waste precious time on the wrong plants for the job.

The Right Plants

Choosing the right plant material for your flower garden means considering not just your garden conditions but also your priorities. For new gardeners speed is often at the top of the list. For quick color

A Self-Seeding Border

This border of annuals, edged with agapanthus, is perfect for the five-minute gardener; it is quickly established and maintains itself. White and pink cleome, white and pale pink cosmos and Queen Anne's Lace are all reliable self-seeders, often establishing a couple of generations in a season.

In moderate areas they will continue flowering all year round, the foliage just yellowing a little in the coldest days of winter.

The tall annuals are fronted by hardy blue agapanthus, whose elegant sword-like foliage hides the messy lower stems of the tall annuals. If planted close together these annuals won't need staking, but they will need lots of sun and the occasional thinning of new crops of seedlings

you can't beat annuals. But for easy care the first choice would be bulbs or perennials. If flexibility is on the list, annuals give you the potential of a whole new look every season. But a little bit of everything, carefully combining a variety of annuals, perennials, and bulbs, gives you the potential for the best garden pictures over the longest time.

Annuals

Annuals are particularly rewarding for the gardener who has just moved into a new house and whose garden must be started from scratch. Annuals grow so fast that you can have a garden filled with flowers just a few weeks after planting. You needn't wait for the landscaping to be done—just plant them where it's convenient and your new house will quickly look lived-in and loved. Annuals only last for one season so when the time comes they can all be swept away to make room for more permanent plantings.

Annuals are also ideal for gardeners who are renting and don't want to invest in shrubs or trees that they can't take with them when they move on. For a few dollars you can plant a flower garden that will make your rented house feel more like home.

Annuals give a big display for a small investment, particularly if you grow them from seed. Some plants grow readily from seed sown where it is to grow in the garden while others need to be in seed boxes and transplanted to the garden later, which puts extra pressure on those minutes you have to spare.

Seedlings, available from nurseries and garden centers, cost a little more than a packet of seeds but save six weeks growing time so are a boon to the five-minute gardener. Best of all though are plants that self-sow readily, providing a new generation of plants, often even before their parents have completely finished flowering.

When they have finished flowering, annuals die off and are pulled up, allowing you to design a new look for the garden every season. Gardening is never boring if it is full of annuals.

The Best Self-Seeding Annuals

Cosmos
Cleome
Flanders poppy
Forget-me-not
Marigold
Nasturtium
Nigella
Primula
Queen Anne's Lace

Perennials

Perennials, on the other hand, take a little longer than annuals to establish themselves, but are equally rewarding as they come up and flower in their season year after year with very little extra effort on the gardener's part. As they are permanent plantings, perennials should be kept to the back of the flower border or in a separate bed where they can remain undisturbed until they need sub-dividing.

The main color display in the autumn garden will come from perennials such as chrysanthemum, dahlia, Easter or Michaelmas daisy (perennial aster), lobelia, penstemon, physostegia, and the perennial sunflower, Helianthus.

In temperate and cool areas the beautiful autumn-flowering windflower

Fast Multiplying Perennials

Alstroemeria	Penstemon	Michaelmas Easter daisy
Oenothera speciosa Rosea	Physostegia (mock erica)	Stoke's aster
Calliopsis	Shasta daisy	Torenia
(Pink evening primrose)	Salvia	Valerian

or Japanese anemone *A x hybrida* will brighten the autumn garden. It will bloom best in part-shade or filtered sunlight, though it does tolerate full sun. There are pure white and pink single and semi-double varieties and a crimson double.

With the exception of the windflower which prefers some shade, the easily-grown perennials mentioned above all need a sunny, well-drained bed and will produce an excellent display of flowers suitable for cutting year after year with very little attention other than normal garden care of watering and feeding.

Some perennials are also good self-seeders, multiplying themselves quickly in a garden bed. Others form clumps quickly that can be divided to further fill the bed and increase the display or to swap for other treasures from like-minded gardeners. This is the kind of shortcut the five-minute gardener is always keen on.

Autumn-flowering perennials need lifting every three years or so when they become overcrowded. The five-minute gardener should not attempt to lift them all the same year—stagger this job so that you deal with, for instance, chrysanthemums one year and Michaelmas daisies another. Dahlias are often lifted each winter but can be left in situ as long as the space they occupy is not needed for other plants.

Tall perennials such as tall dahlias and the taller-growing chrysanthemums will give much better results if they are staked. This is best done at planting time to avoid damage to roots.

If you have extra bulbs and containers, make further plantings a few weeks after your first planting so you will enjoy a succession of flowers rather than a single impressive burst.

Bulbs

Bulbs are also great value for the five-minute gardener. In the picking garden they can be planted in rows for easy cutting, but in the flower garden, plant them in clumps among spring annuals for a more attractive effect. Bulbs are also excellent container plants and can be grown on sunny balconies and patios and for a decorative effect (beside steps or an ornamental pool for instance) in the garden.

In fact, bulbs that are marginal in your climate (tulips, daffodils, and hyacinths in warm winter areas, for instance) are often better grown in a container to get full enjoyment from them for their one season of flowering. If you decide to attempt marginal bulbs in a warm or tropical climate, it is best to regard them as annuals. They are not good value for the five-minute gardener, but are fun to try.

Of all the spring-flowering bulbs, ranunculas and anemones will give the most rewarding results for the five-minute gardener. Masses of blooms spring from the tiny, wrinkled claws and corms and they will do well in all areas. In sandy soils plant them a little deeper than in more loamy soils and put a handful of mulch over the soil surface after planting. This will protect bulbs from heating up and being damaged in the sandy soils.

Forcing Bulbs Indoors

Some bulbs can be forced indoors and this is great fun for the five-minute gardener who gardens in a small space, a courtyard, or on a balcony or patio. Young children also love watching flowers bloom from these unlikely beginnings.

Hyacinths can be grown in a bulb glass that is filled with water with the bulb sitting on top so that the base of the bulb is just clear of the water. Place it in a dark, cool cupboard until roots grow and a shoot appears, then transfer the glass and bulb gradually (over a week) to a better light and then on to a well-lit but cool windowsill where the flower stem will quickly grow and bloom.

After flowering, bulbs grown indoors must be discarded or planted out in the garden to recover as they will be exhausted and won't reflower indoors.

Narcissus can also be forced but are better grown in a bowl filled with bulb fiber. The bulb fiber is moistened thoroughly but should not be dripping wet. Plant the bulbs with the necks showing above the fiber. Place in a cool, dark cupboard and follow the same method as for hyacinths to get a dramatic effect in quick time.

Check the bulb fiber regularly and water gently when dry. It is

Color

One of the pleasures of growing annual flowers is that it is easy to plan a color scheme that can be changed each season. Many of the bedding plants, such as petunias, violas, and primula, are sold in pots in separate colors.

To achieve the best effect with your color scheme, consider plant size as well as flower color. Annuals range in height from ground covers, such as alyssum, to plants of medium height (2–5 feet/.5m–.75m), such as stocks and Iceland poppies, through to quite tall, bushy plants up to 6½ feet (2m) tall, such as hollyhocks, dahlias, and sunflowers.

Include plants of each size to give height and balance to the garden. Tall plants should be planted where they won't shade the smaller flowers and sometimes need a spot where they get sun but are protected from strong winds. The lowest growers make great edgings and are useful to spill over and soften garden edges.

important not to add too much water if you are using a bowl without a drainage hole. A layer of gravel or pebbles and a piece of charcoal in the base of the bowl will help overcome the problem of too much moisture, but always drain the bowl by tilting it, with your hand held over the top to prevent pebbles or bulbs from spilling, to ensure there is no surplus water in the bottom which could rot your bulbs.

You can also grow bulbs on pebbles. You will need a container 4–5 inches (10–12cm) deep (oval bonsai dishes are excellent, also deep glass containers). Place a layer of pebbles in the base and add water almost to the top of the pebbles. Stand bulbs close together but not quite touching, on top of the pebbles but not touching the water. Then finish filling the container with pebbles until just the neck of the bulbs remains clear.

The pebbles will give necessary support to the bulbs as they grow taller so that they don't topple over. Follow the cool dark treatment as described above. The roots will grow down to the water in the bottom of the container and as the plants grow they will absorb more moisture. Add extra water carefully when necessary to prevent drying out.

Fragrance

Perfume is an important part of the enjoyment of a flower garden. Many of the fragrant plants are at their most perfumed at dusk when you can sit out in the cool of the

Design for a Daisy Bed

There are lots of flowers we call daisies which aren't strictly daisies but have the sunny, open-faced flowers typical of the daisy. One of the time-honored design principles is that like goes with like, so that a flower bed of daisies, whether they are true daisies of the family Asteraceae or not, is sure to be a success. And, given that most daisies are very easy to grow and have few requirements, they are ideal five-minute garden material.

Some daisies, such as marguerite, which is actually a chrysanthemum (Chrysanthemum frutescens), make great informal hedges, along the front fence of a cottage-style house, for example. The Parisian daisy, Europs, with its bright yellow flowers and silvery-blue foliage is also popular in block plantings.

The casual friendliness is celebrated in all sorts of cottage gardens, but daisies also have a place in more formal arrangements.

The design for a daisy bed shown to the right limits the daisy color wheel to white, blue, and yellow. The focus of this semi-circular bed is a sundial, to remind us that what daisies like best is lots of sun.

Also featured are:

1. White marguerite daisies (Chrysanthemum frutescens)
2. Europs
3. Aster frikartii
4. White shasta daisies (Chrysanthemum maximum)
5. Yellow everlasting daisy (Helichrysum bracteatum)
6. Stokesia
7. Swan river daisy (Brachycome iberidifolia)
8. Poached egg flower (Limnanthes douglasii)

1
2
3
4
5
6
7
8
6

evening marveling at the success of your five-minute flower garden. Choose from fragrant annuals, such as lupins, alyssum, carnation, pinks, pansy, wallflower, sweet pea, mignonette, stock, petunia, and phlox.

Shrubs

To complement your five-minute flower garden and give it a framework, you could add some easy-care flowering shrubs that will give your garden year-round flowers without too much help from you.

The shrubs you select will depend on your space, climate, and soil, but there are many that can be grown in gardens everywhere—roses for instance, can be grown in most gardens, from the tropics to cold areas.

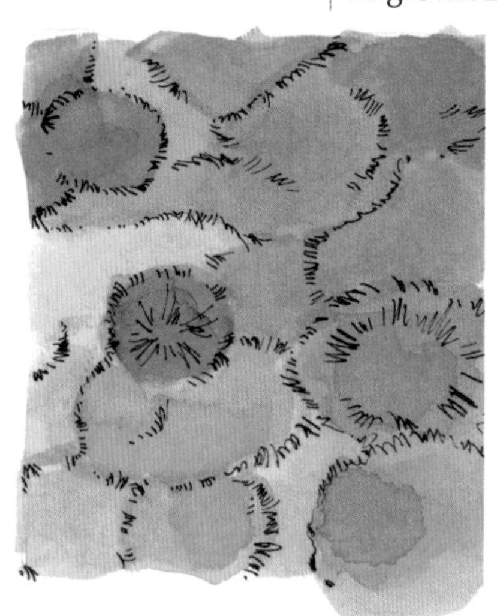

Gardeners in frost-free coastal areas will find that they have a very wide choice of shrubs; much the same shrubs can be grown right around the coast.

The five-minute gardener in a frost-prone garden can still grow hibiscus, but the deciduous Syrian hibiscus *H. syriacus*, rather than the frost-tender *H. rosa-sinensis*, is the right choice. Though the color range of flowers is more limited—mainly white, mauve, and crimson

Shrubs for Autumn Flowers

Camellia sasanqua
Gordonia
Hibiscus mutabilis (rose of Sharon)
Justicia
Luculia
Plectranthus
Poinsettia
Salvia leucantha (Mexican sage)
Tibouchina

Shrubs for Winter Flowers

Azalea
Buddleia salvifolia (sage-leaf buddleia)
Camellia japonica
Chamelaucium uncinatum (geraldton wax)
Daphne
Euryops
Prunus mume (flowering apricot)
French lavender
Garrya
Iboza riparia (nutmeg bush)
Reinwardtia (golden dollar plant)
Ruellia
Strelitzia (bird of paradise flower)
Winter sweet (cold climates only)
Witch hazel (cold climates only)
Tibouchina

Shrubs for Spring Flowers

Azalea
Banksia rose
Browallia
Brunfelsia
Camellia
Ceanothus (cool areas only)
Coleonema
Fuchsia (temperate and cool areas)
Lilac (temperate and cool areas)
Magnolia (temperate areas)
Spiraea (May)
Philadelphus
Pieris (temperate to cool areas)
Rhodondrendron (temperate to cool)
Rondeletia
Spartium junceum (Spanish broom)
Viburnum

Shrubs for Frost-free Gardens and Near-Year-Round Flowers

Abelia
Abutilon
Beloperone (shrimp plant)
Bougainvillea
Clerodendrum ugandense (butterfly bush)
Ceratostigma willmottianum (Chinese plumbago or skybush)
Crape myrtle
Crown of thorns*
Cuphea *
Duranta
Felicia *
Fuchsia (temperate to cool areas only)
Gardenia
Grevillea (named hybrids)
Hebe*
Heliotrope *
Hibiscus
Hydrangea (part-shade)
Hypericum
Mussaenda (especially M. philippica 'Buddha's Lamp', 'Queen Sirikit' and 'Gining Imelda', for warm to tropical areas)
Oleander
Pentas *
Plumbago
Plumeria (Frangipani)
Pomegranate
Rose
Russelia *
Tecoma
Tecomaria
Tibouchina
Vitex

* small shrubs growing to less than 3 feet (1m). Also look for dwarf forms of Abutilon, crepe myrtle, pomegranate, rose, and Tibouchina.

colors—the Syrian hibiscus is tough and just as attractive and free-flowering as the Chinese species.

The secret for success in growing shrubs for a flower-filled garden all year is careful selection. Leave the tricky or tender plants to someone with more time to cosset, coddle, and coax reluctant plants. And in planning for non-stop color, make sure you choose a least one shrub to be at its best in each season.

When planting labor-saving shrubs take care to find out how wide and tall they are likely to grow and allow them enough space to reach those dimensions. Otherwise constant clipping and pruning will be needed.

When ordering soil it will help you to work out quantities if you estimate that 35 cubic feet (1 cubic meter) = 1 ton of soil.

A Mound Garden

A level site is the easiest to garden but mystery and surprise are hard to maintain on the flat garden. The quickest way to add visual interest, and plenty of flowers, is with a mound.

A mound garden is simple to achieve with little more than a load of good garden soil. It is preferable for you to take the soil from somewhere in your own garden. This will ensure

A Mound Garden

When you plan your mound garden it is important to remember that as the soil settles down the volume, therefore the size of the mound, will reduce over a short period of time. Make the mound larger than you need, to allow for shrinkage. If you are buying soil from a garden supplier, they will help you determine the amount of soil you will need, including extra for volume loss.

that the soil will maintain the nutrients necessary for your mound garden to be productive year after year. However, if this is not possible, garden suppliers have an excellent choice of friable, humus-rich soils to choose from. A mound garden should be at least 3 feet (1m) wide by 3 feet (1m) high and can be any shape—a round or curving island bed set in the lawn, or a long bed running along the front of the property on the boundary, where it will not only provide a wonderful splash of color but add privacy and act as a noise buffer.

Laying newspaper is easiest if you wet it first with the hose or dunk it into a tub of water. The wet paper clings together and stays put on the ground. The newspaper should be about ½-inch (1cm) thick—the sections the paper usually divides into—i.e. sports/advertising/news/travel—is usually a suitable thickness when well overlapped.

A mound garden can also be an advantage if you have a problem with the soil—poor drainage, shallow soil, heavy clay, or sand—you simply build up and away from the problem and plant your favorite flowers and shrubs.

No digging is involved in creating a mound garden. If your chosen site is covered with grass or weeds, put well-overlapped newspapers down first to suppress growth. If you prefer, pull out the big guns and spray the area with Roundup to kill any existing grass or weeds. Follow the chemicals with a layer of newspaper mulch to suppress any growth that might survive the weed-killer. Bulb-like perennial weeds like nut-grass, oxalis, and onion

If building an island flower bed in lawn without a mower strip, spray or paint around the edging with a natural herbicide to kill the grass which may otherwise creep through into the garden and need to be weeded out. You'll need to spray a couple of times through the summer. The procedure will leave a narrow strip of brown grass 1 inch (3–4cm) wide.

grass tend to grow up again from detached juvenile or dormant bulbs that were not affected by the poison absorbed by the main root or bulb.

Mark out the shape of curved or free-form mound beds with a plastic garden hose or use a length of string and pegs for straight lines. Trace the outline around the hose or along the string line with lime or with a dribble of weed-killer.

While garden edgings are not essential for a mound garden, an edging and mower strip will make control of grass much easier if your mound is an island in a sea of lawn.

Mound the soil so that it falls in a natural way, playing mother nature in miniature as you form slopes, peaks, and minor valleys so that your mound doesn't look as if it was simply tipped out of the trailer. Rake it smooth before planting.

The resulting formation can be planted in two ways, either by completely over-sowing with seeds that will grow where they are sown and keeping the mound lightly watered until germination, or by planting out a selection of seedlings, then sprinkling seeds in between for a more completely flowery mass.

An early spring planting of seeds of annuals such as cosmos, cleome, Californian poppy, Queen Anne's lace, and others will give a wonderful display.

A Picking Garden

Another way to develop a five-minute flower patch is to make a picking garden in a sunny part of your backyard next to the vegetable garden, or instead of the vegetable garden if you feel like a change.

A picking garden was a regular feature of the home garden in times past when people had more leisure both to grow and arrange flowers and it is still essential for people who enjoy cutting blooms for the house. With a little planning, a picking garden is not too difficult for the five-minute flower gardener.

The picking garden is planted in rows for ease of picking. It isn't meant to look particularly ornamental (apart from being neat and tidy) and is put into the practical part of the garden along with the compost heap, fruit trees, and vegetables.

Mark out rows evenly just as you would for vegetables. It is best for beds to run north/south so that plants get maximum sunlight. On sloping sites the beds will need to be made across

PLENTY OF SUN

A picking garden requires full sun. Flowers that are shaded will lean and won't have the strong, straight stems necessary for flower arrangements.

A bale or two of spoiled alfalfa hay or straw is a great asset to the five-minute picking gardener. You will have a source of extra mulch for the path when it needs another layer in wet weather and hay or straw is an excellent mulch to run between the rows of plants to keep down weeds and keep the soil from drying out too quickly.

Flowers for Picking

Aster
Candytuft (hyacinth-flowered type)
Canterbury bells
Carnation
Chrysanthemum
Cornflower
Cosmos
Dahlia
Delphinium
Dianthus
Everlasting daisy
Gerbera
Gypsophila
Irish green bellflower
Larkspur
Lupin
Marmalade daisy
Nigella
Poppy
Queen Anne's lace
Snapdragon
Statice
Stock
Sweet pea
Wallflower
Zinnia

Flowers for Drying

Everlasting daisies
Statice
Linaria
Honesty (seed pods)
Gypsophila

the slope with a low retaining wall to contain the soil.

Where the soil is heavy the soil level should be raised by 6 to 8 inches (16 to 20cm) by the addition of plenty of old manure, compost, spent mushroom compost, peat (or preferably a peat substitute such as coco-peat) and good garden soil to ensure good drainage.

Depending on the space you have available, the picking garden might be a long bed about 3 feet (1m) wide, or a large square, divided into 3 feet (1m) wide strips by a path just wide enough to walk on.

Cover the access strip with a thick layer of straw or leaf litter to suppress weeds and to keep your feet from getting wet and muddy.

Light sands soils will need exactly the same additions to improve the water-holding capacity of the soil, prevent drying out, and encourage earthworm activity. If you live near the coast, seaweed makes a wonderful addition to sandy soils and is free for the gathering.

To keep your picking garden producing flowers, stagger the plantings over a few weeks in the same way as you would vegetables to spread the harvest time. This can be done either by planting extra pots of seedlings at two weekly intervals or by sowing an extra row of seeds when the previous sowing has developed true leaves.

The picking garden may also need a trellis, particularly if you wish to grow sweet peas—and who wouldn't? With their beautiful scent, luscious range of colors, and habit of increasing flowering as picked, the sweet pea is one of the most important flowers

If you use the square bed pattern divided by narrow, straw, or mulch-covered access paths, these paths will supply some rich compost by the end of the season. This can be spaded onto the beds and fresh straw put down to cover the path, or the beds themselves can be moved over an inch or so (2–4cm) to incorporate the path and take advantage of the soil which has been enriched by the composted mulch.

Where there is no space for a trellis, sweet peas can be grown on a tripod—use three hardwood garden stakes or bamboo if you have a supply. Push stakes firmly into the soil and latch together at the top. Wrap plastic mesh, plastic string, or wire around the stakes to provide climbing support.

of the cutting garden. The trellis should be placed beside the main flower bed where it will not shade other plants. Putting up the trellis will require a little extra work, but if you put in two (or more if the trellis is long) permanent support posts which can be left in position, you will only need to fasten up a length of plastic trellis (much easier to handle than wire-netting) when you prepare the bed for planting seed.

Though a picking garden can consist entirely of annuals, the keen arranger may want to incorporate a few rose bushes and a few favorite, but easily-grown perennials that do well in the area.

Some perennials, such as a row of blue and white agapanthus, will provide good cut flowers for summer with almost no attention. Roses do require some extra care so don't plant too many (the more plants you have, the more pests and diseases will be attracted to them) and select only strong-growing, disease-resistant varieties with flowers on long, strong stems which hold well when cut. A rose catalog from your nearest rose nursery will list roses recommended for cutting.

Sun Jewels

Long life in the vase isn't the only reason to choose a flowering plant. Some plants give a good flower display, but aren't suitable for picking because they have short stems. Others fall rapidly or close up out of the sun. Winter/spring-flowering Livingstone daisy and the summer-flowering Portulaca are good examples of this type of flower but they have the big plus of giving a brilliant show in full sun in the garden. Sun Jewels is a perennial Portulaca, which does not close on dull days and flowers for months in warm climates. This makes a superb hanging basket in full sun. It also brightens the edge of a raised garden where it will trail a brilliant shawl of color.

Portulaca

Roses for Picking

Avon - red
Champagner - creamy
Blue Moon - mauve-blue
Holtermann's Gold - yellow
Kardinal - red
Lagerfeld - silvery lilac-blue
Peter Frankenfeld - pink
Sonia - soft coral
Touch of Class - coral pink
Valerie Swane - white

If your picking garden is a great success, you might likely to make it more than a hobby by supplying cut flowers to your local florist, a local store, coffee shop, or perhaps a stall at a local street market. Bunches of seasonal flowers such as carnations, chrysanthemums, gladiolus, daffodils, statice, and baby's breath are usually in demand. Cottage bunches or small posies are also a popular item at the corner store on Fridays. Selling a few flowers from your five-minute flower patch might bring in enough money to pay for the next batch of seedlings or packet of seeds. The biggest demand for your flowers will probably be from committees organizing contributions to fund-raising functions. The five-minute flower patch is primarily for fun, not profit.

Special Garden Conditions

The Shady Flower Garden

If there is no convenient space in your garden that gets the six hours of sun a day necessary for a successful planting of sun-loving flowers, you can still achieve a five-minute flower patch by growing plants that will thrive in partial shade or filtered sunlight.

Do not attempt a flower garden in full shade since most flowering plants need some sunlight to grow. If you have deciduous trees, take advantage of their deciduous period, when plenty of sun shines through the bare branches, to grow spring flowering bulbs and flowers, moving into more shade-loving plants as the canopy thickens in the summer.

In Spring

One of the ideal spring-flowering bulbs for areas shaded by deciduous trees or shrubs is *Leucojum vernum* (snowflake), which grows and flowers over a wide climate range. It is ideal for the five-minute gardener as it can be left in the ground without the trouble of lifting each year and has a long flowering period from January to March.

Snowflake has white cup-shaped bells with a green spot on each petal and the flower stems rise from clumps of glossy green foliage.

Other suitable bulbs include bluebell, grape

Definitions of Shady

Filtered sun: The sun is broken by foliage or by shade-cloth.

Part-shade: The position is at times in full sun but is shaded at other parts of the day by trees or by the house and/or other buildings.

Full shade: Never gets direct sun.

The five-minute gardener in warmer climates should concentrate on the South African bulbs, which include freesia, ixia, ifafa lily, babiana, gladiolus, sparaxis, and watsonia. These will flower reliably, while the more temperate bulbs can be disappointing after the first year, growing but not flowering.

A little snail bait sprinkled around clivia plants when the buds begin to appear will ensure a good display.

hyacinth, narcissus, jonquil, and daffodil, which need temperate to cool climates. Freesia, sparaxis, ixia, triteleia, and tritonia will naturalize in temperate to warm areas and reward the gardener with trouble-free flowers through spring.

The old-fashioned cream and white freesias will grow in light shade and are a better choice than modern hybrids which have long stems and need plenty of direct sun to encourage upright growth. Old-fashioned *F. refracta* will naturalize freely and perfume the air.

Clivia is an easily grown perennial for shady areas. It has dark green strap-like leaves year-round and large, showy salmon heads of lilies in late winter and spring. Clivia suits the five-minute gardener as it can be left undisturbed for many years, requires little maintenance and the long-lasting flowers can be picked.

Winter/spring annuals that will do well in a garden bed receiving sunlight through bare branches include dwarf ageratum, cineraria, primula, polyanthus, Bellis perennis, forget-me-not, and cynoglossum (hound's tongue).

Forget-me-Not

Foxgloves, which grow

Annuals for Part-shade or Filtered Sun

- Ageratum
- Cineraria
- Columbine
- Bedding begonia
- Calceolaria
- Coleus (grown for foliage)
- Bellis perennis (English daisy)
- Forget-me-not
- Foxglove (must have some full morning sun)
- Heart's ease or Johnny-jump-up
- Impatiens (pictured)
- Linaria
- Lobelia
- Nasturtium
- Polyanthus
- Primrose
- Primula
- Schizanthus
- Torenia

strongly through spring but don't flower until early summer, will do well in this position provided you plant them at the outer edge of the shady area where they will continue to get some sun at flowering time when the trees are in full leaf. In too much shade their stems lean forward to the light and are weak.

There are some small, shrubby plants that are good value for the shaded five-minute flower garden. Brazilian plume flower, *Justicia carnea* has flesh-pink flower plumes in late summer. Libonia *J.rizzinii*, has yellow-tipped, scarlet tubular blooms and forms a sprawling plant, 3 feet by 4½ feet (1m x 1.5m), with the main flower flush in winter and spring but intermittently at other times. Both plants perform well with ordinary garden care plus a little snail bait to protect the leaves.

In Summer

During summer, when your flower bed is shaded by the leafy canopy of deciduous trees, you could do worse than concentrate on the reliable Busy Lizzie—there are many dwarf and hybrid varieties in bright colors with single or double flowers. (Incidentally many of the modern varieties grow well in full sun, provided they are well watered.) As a background to these flowers, search out Iresine. This is a small plant that is grown for its leaf color rather than for its flowers. It retains its green and deep red or yellow color when grown in shade.

Butterfly impatiens and Busy Lizzie are sold as advanced plants in bloom for an instant effect—another plus for the five-minute gardener.

For a garden bed that gets some morning sun, try the New Guinea butterfly impatiens. These are larger than the usual Busy Lizzie and have colorful foliage which needs several hours of morning sun to bring out the full color, and very large, showy flowers.

Gardeners used to the usual Busy Lizzie often make the mistake of planting the New Guinea butterfly impatiens in shade. However, in too much shade they quickly lose their leaf color and stop flowering. If this happens, move them into morning sun (hot afternoon sun causes rapid wilting), water frequently, and feed.

Another summer-flowering plant for part-shade or filtered sun which is not as well known as it should be is the Chinese foxglove, *Rehmannia*. This charming plant has large, soft leaves and sends up stems of lavender bells somewhat reminiscent of foxgloves. It looks handsome in the garden and can be used to give height among lower growing flowers. It is usually available as an advanced plant in bloom, but has also recently become available in pots.

The Chinese poppy or snowpoppy, *Eomecon,* is also little known and loves damp shade. It is a perennial with heart-shaped leaves and stems of snow-white poppy flowers throughout the year. It's a great colonizer under trees or on banks, and so is the much better known nasturtium. Nasturtiums will scramble around happily in filtered sun or part shade. If in too much shade, however, the flowers will tend to be obscured by the leaves. Grow nasturtiums hard for a good show of

Perennials for Part-shade or Filtered

Ajuga
Arum
Eomecon (snow poppy or Chinese poppy)
Hellebore
Hosta
Primrose
Polyanthus
Polygonatum multiflorum (Solomon's seal)
Violet
Vinca minor
Cyclamen sp. (cool climate only)
Autumn crocus (cool climate only)
Lily-of-the-valley (cool climate only)

flowers—liberal amounts of fertilizer and water result in lots of leaf growth at the expense of flowers.

Some ground-covering plants that will give a good flower display in filtered shade include ajuga, lamium, and vinca.

These are best in temperate to cool areas, while in warm to tropical areas try the Philippine violet, barleria.

If you have damp shade, even a positively boggy spot, go for permanent clumps of arum lilies, including the striking green goddess. These are splendid cut flowers and make the ideal filler for the five-minute gardener. Once planted they seldom need any attention at all.

The Hot Flower Garden

If your five-minute flower patch is in full sun, or gets at least six hours of full sun a day, you can enjoy a riot of easy color—ageratum, alyssum, aster, balsam, bedding begonia, California poppy, cleome, cosmos, gypsophila, kochia, marigold, nasturtium, petunia, phlox, portulaca, rudbeckia, salvia, salpiglossis, snapdragon, sunflower, and zinnia will all thrive.

Seeds or bedding plants are sown in spring—in warm to tropical, frost-free areas earlier plantings can be made to beat the mid-summer heat. Advanced bedding plants can be planted until early July to fill spaces and keep the display going into autumn.

For easy color, don't overlook the perennial

A Crinum for All Climates

There are some summer-flowering bulbs that relish filtered sunlight or partial shade. These include the crinums, white or pink lilies that are available in several excellent species suitable for all climates. Crinums are permanent plants, having large bulbs that can be left to slowly form clumps.

Crinum moorei and *C. x powellii* have tall stems bearing clusters of large pink or white, drooping bells, which are good cut flowers. They enjoy morning sun or filtered sunlight.

The poison lily, *C. asiaticum*, is popular with gardeners in warm to tropical climates and will grow in full sun, partial sun, or filtered sun. It has heads of white spider lilies and clumps of green foliage, yellow in sun, often planted as a dwarf hedge in tropical and sub-tropical gardens.

The native Darling lily, *C. flaccidum*, also with large heads of white spider flowers, makes a splendid architectural statement in a partly shaded corner or under a tree.

All crinums are fragrant, make good cut flowers and need little care—perfect for the five-minute gardener.

For the tropical and sub-tropical gardener, clumps of ginger lilies, lobster claws, *Heliconia sp.*, and blue ginger, *Dichorisandra*, will also thrive in filtered sun with summer moisture. The yellow ginger lily; *Hedychium gardenerianum*, is widely grown even in temperate coastal gardens. It is fragrant and makes a good cut flower.

Every five-minute gardener in a warm tropical climate should have some plants of granny's bonnet, *Angelonia*. This small, dainty perennial sends up stems of flowers that look like miniature penstemons all through the year in warm areas. The species is mauve and white, but new forms are now available in a range of blue/mauve/white and pink. Very easy to grow and suffering no pests or diseases, this old favorite can be picked.

Celosia and gomphrena make great flowering pot plants on a hot, sunny balcony or patio.

vinca, *Catharanthus roseus* syn. *Vinca rosea*. This plant flowers in the hottest weather is available in a range of pretty, named compact varieties in white, pink, and mauve colors.

Most summer annuals grow well in every climate but if you live in the subtropical to tropical zones, you will get great results from the members of the Amaranthus family, such as Joseph's coat, grown for its brilliantly colored foliage; love-lies-bleeding, with its long tassels of chenille-like flowers (also in yellow-green varieties, viridis and green pearls); cockscomb, celosia, with crested feathery flowers; and globe amaranth or batchelor's buttons, *Gomphrena*, with its bright clover-like flower heads.

Salvia splendens, often known as bonfire salvia, is another first-rate color-maker for the hottest spots. Now available in a range of colors including purple, crimson, salmon, rose, white, and bicolor as well as the original scarlet, salvia forms a shrubby plant to 24 inches (60cm) (dwarf forms are also

Salvia

available) and stands up well to hot, dry conditions. Salvia flowers for months and, cut back after the main flush, will give another long burst of color and in most gardens a second prune will result in another flowering the following year.

In hot summer gardens cannas will also give a brilliant show. Don't waste time with weedy old species, buy modern hybrids—the dwarf varieties are excellent for the flower garden. Flowers come in a range of vivid colors and some have bronze or variegated foliage, which is a bonus. Cannas are perennials and the only work involved is in cutting them back after flowering has finished. Any garden soil with regular garden watering will give great results.

Gardeners in hot, dry summer climates where humidity is low will enjoy a good display of plants such as aster and zinnia, which can develop mildew in humid summers. Petunias also thrive without the threat of gray mold fungus, which can damage

Some plants of the blue and white varieties of *Salvia farinacea* can be grown with the bonfire salvias to add the cool and refreshing touch of blue and white to the color scheme.

In cold districts or if hosts are likely, care for your cannas by mulching right over the crowns with a thick layer of straw or leaf mulch.

plantings in humid, coastal gardens.

Zinnias will tolerate any amount of heat and give a long and very rewarding display of flowers, which are excellent for cutting. There is a delightful rockery zinnia known as Little Star. *Angustifolia syn. linearis*, which has small, bright golden flowers and is now also available in white. The five-minute gardener will love this plant—it flowers for several months, thrives in hot, dry conditions and suits rockeries, garden edgings and containers.

In cold districts or if hosts are likely, care for your cannas by mulching right over the crowns with a thick layer of straw or leaf mulch.

The Seaside Flower Garden

Many people garden by the sea in sandy soil and often have to contend with salty sea breezes, if the garden is very exposed to the salty wind, a protective barrier planting will be essential for success—a row of salt-resistant shrubs, such as coast rosemary, *Westringia fruticosa*, or coastal tea-tree provides good protection without obscuring views.

Escalonia, with dense green foliage and pink,

red, or white flowers for most of the year, is also an excellent choice for the seaside garden. For more savage conditions you might have to resort to *Cupressis macrocarpa,* which is often used in Victoria, Australia where winds blow straight from Antarctica.

Annuals for Hot Humid Gardens

Amaranthus
Angelonia
Celosia
Gomphrena
Torenia
Nasturtium

Annuals for Hot Dry Gardens

Alyssum
Cosmos
Marigold
Portulaca
Bonfire salvia
Stocks
Vinca
Catharanthus (Madigascar periwinkle)
Zinnia
* regular watering over root area will give the best results

When making new plantings, add one of the commercial water crystals to the bottom of the planting hole and water well. The crystals will absorb water that the plant roots can tap in dry times. Adding water crystals will increase your success rate dramatically.

Seaweed can be used straight from the beach on seaside gardens. No preparation is necessary.

The five-minute gardener by the seaside should prepare the garden thoroughly before planting, digging in plenty of compost, leaf mulch, manure (basically anything old and organic) to the top 6 inches (15cm) of sand. This will help hold moisture and fertilizer and save a lot of time in watering and feeding. After planting, add mulch over the surface (seaweed is great on sandy soils) to help keep the roots cool (sandy soils heat up quickly on hot summer days).

There are plenty of easily grown flowering annuals for sandy conditions—anything with daisy flowers, plants with woolly, gray, or silvery foliage, glossy or waxy foliage that resists salt or succulent leaves and stems will do well.

Small shrubby plants such as lavender, marguerite daisy, Dietes, prostrate lavender lantana, *L. montevidensis*, and new lantana varieties white lightning (white flowers) and lavender swirl (pink, white, and lilac) and named lantana hybrids in pink,

Flowers for Seaside

Agapanthus
Alyssum
Angelonia (granny's bonnets)
Arctotis (Aurora daisy)
California poppy
Calliopsis
Cleome
Cosmos
Daisies (everlasting, flannel flower, marguerite, Shasta, Brachycome, Felicia, Euryops)
Gaillardia
Gazania
Pelargonium
Gerbera
Livingstone daisy
Lupin
Petunia
Lampranthus (pigface)
Lavender
Nasturtium
Portulaca
Pride of Madeira
Rosemary
Oenothera speciosa
Rudbeckia
Statice
Stock
Vinca (Madagascar periwinkle, Catharanthus roseus, now available in good named dwarf forms such as Pretty in Pink)

cream, gold, scarlet, and orange shades, will give a constant succession of garden flowers.

The stately perennial forms of pride of Madeira, *Echium fastuosum*, and the pink-flowered *E. wildpretii*, will add dramatic spires of color. These plants are not like the weed species known variously as Salvation Jane and Patterson's Curse and will not become a pest. They are easy to grow and are trouble-free in sandy or well-drained soils in inland as well as seaside gardens.

Where summer storms are a hazard to the flower garden, the five-minute gardener could plant Torenia, a tough and flowery little annual from Vietnam that can stand up to rain, humidity, and storms and come up smiling. Mainly blue with darker blue blotches and a yellow throat (var. Little Gem), Torenia can sometimes be found in the more recent Clown Mix which produces flowers in a variety of pink, mauve, and blue all with white highlights.

Torenia will grow in full sun or part-shade, in the garden or in containers and will self-sow happily—a plus for the five-minute gardener.

The Holiday House Garden

A holiday house garden only receives intermittent care at weekends or during holidays but you can still have a flowery garden on the five-minute principle if you plant a few hardy shrubs. Choose from allamanda, hibiscus, oleander, plumbago and native banksia and coastal wattles; perennial daisies such as gaillardia and marguerite; flannel flowers, prostrate lantana (including the new named varieties), geraniums, native golden guinea flower, *Hibbertia scandens*, which can be used as a mounding, trailing, or ground-covering plant and is native to the dunes. Try to avoid a conventional lawn that will need constant mowing. Use ground-covering plants instead, such as dichondra, scaevola or *Coprosma x kirkii* and rely where possible on any existing native grasses. Try to do most of the planting when you are going to be staying for a couple of weeks so that you can give the new residents some watering to get them established. Mulch generously so that they will survive your absence.

Planting

The work you put into preparing your flower bed before planting will show up later in healthier plants which will produce better blooms. The key is using lots of organic matter to make a rich source of food for your flowers.

Layer well-rotted manure or compost over the soil and add a complete fertilizer at the rate of 1/2 tablespoon per square foot (one third of a cup per square meter). Fork or rake it all lightly into the top 5 inches (12cm) of soil. Water and then leave the flower bed for at least a week to allow any weeds to germinate. Pull out or scuff over annual weeds, but take care to remove all parts of the pesky perennials, such as oxalis and onion weed.

Do not over-fertilize the soil as this will promote excessive leaf growth at the expense of flowers.

Heavy or acid soils will benefit from a dressing of lime or dolomite sprinkled over the top of the soil. Calculate1½ tablespoons to the square foot (1 cup to the square meter) for heavy or salt-affected soils but otherwise 1 tablespoon per square foot (half a

A Preparation Timetable
1. Fork manure and complete fertilizer into the soil, taking care not to dig deeply into the subsoil.
2. Water the bed.
3. Wait at least a week for weeds to germinate; rake over annual weeds, and carefully pull out perennials.

4. Add gypsum if soil is heavy.

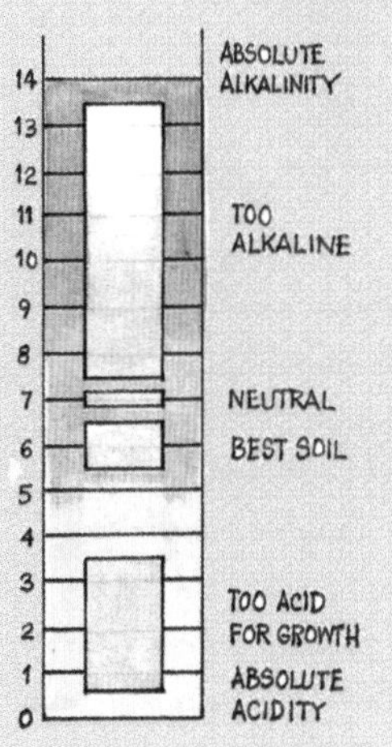

5. Check pH. Aim for a reading of 6 or 7. Add lime or dolomite to overly acid soils (under 5.5) and sulphur to overly alkaline soils (over 7.5).

6. Rake until smooth and even ready for sowing or planting of seedlings.

If your soil is clayey and heavy to dig; if it dries out and forms a crust; or remains wet for long periods after rain, a liberal dressing of gypsum watered and forked through will help to make it more friable. It will become more water-absorbent and easier to work. Gypsum is a soil conditioner and does not effect pH of the soil as lime does.

cup per square meter) will be sufficient. This can be done when adding the compost and fertilizer. Some gardeners like to add lime one week after the fertilizer, but this adds to the waiting time. For most soils it is not necessary to add lime every year. If planting sweet peas, however, which enjoy a slightly alkaline soil, it is usual to sprinkle a dusting of lime along the rows as a pre-planting treatment.

If you are not certain whether your soil is acid or alkaline you can obtain a simple soil-testing kit from most nurseries. Most plants will grow in soil that is very slightly acid—a pH of between 6.0 and 7.0. A quick clue to pH can be gained from hydrangeas growing in your own or nearby gardens—pink hydrangeas indicate alkaline soil—blue ones mean the soil is acid.

Having prepared the bed, you're ready to plant. Best planting times are autumn for winter and spring flowers, and spring for summer and autumn flowers.

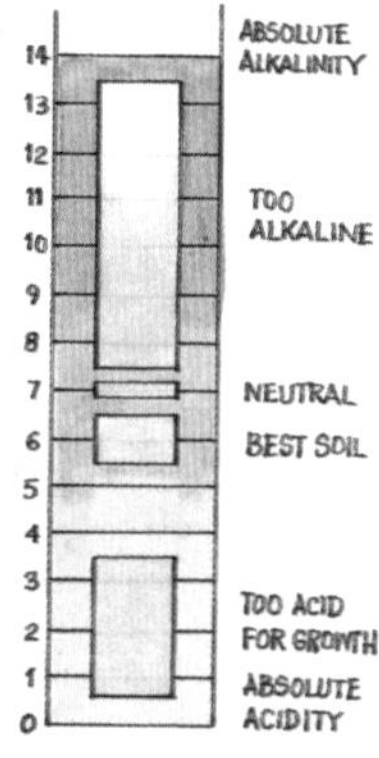

Autumn Plantings

Autumn is the big planting season for the flower gardener. As the summer annuals finish, pull them up and put them into the compost. The five-minute gardener can't waste time on plants that have finished their season. It is time to make way for the bulbs and annuals that will flower in spring and even in winter in mild coastal climates. Gardeners in temperate and cool areas will start their autumn planting in September. However, in warm to tropical zones it is better to wait until the weather cools down in October or November.

Autumn Annuals

Alyssum
Bellis perennis (English daisy)
Calendula
Candytuft
Canterbury bell
Carnation
Cineraria
Columbine
Cornflower
Delphinium
Dianthus
Everlasting daisy
Forget-me-not
Foxglove
Green Irish bells
Gypsophila
Honesty
Larkspur
Leptosyne
Linaria
Livingstone daisy
Lobelia
Lupin
Marigold
Mignonette
Nasturtium
Nemesia
Nemophila
Painted daisy
Pansy
Penstemon
Polyanthus primrose
Poppy (Iceland, Shirley, Flanders)
Primula
Schizanthus
Snapdragon
Sweet pea
Strawflower
Stock
Verbena

Autumn Bulbs

Allium
Alstroemeria
Anemone
Babiana
Bluebell
Brodiaea
Clivia
Daffodil
Dutch iris
Freesia
Grape hyacinth
Ifafa lily
Ixia
Ipheion (also sold as triteleia or blue star flower)
Gladiolus sp.
Jonquil
Lachenalia
Narcissus
Lilium longiflorum (Easter lily)
Ranunculus
Snowflake
Sparaxis
Tritonia
Tulip
Watsonia
Cold climates only
Chionodoxa (glory of the snow)
Crocus
Erythronium (trout lily)
Fritillaria

Winter Plantings

Winter plantings of annuals in most climates will be limited to replacements to fill spaces left by failed or spent plants. In warm temperate areas, though, pots of seedlings are available throughout the winter. Give extra waterings with half-strength liquid fertilizers to late plantings to help them catch up with earlier plantings.

In warm and tropical, frost-free areas winter is often the best time to plant as the weather is kinder and this is when advanced seedlings are available in good condition.

Winter is a good planting time for a whole range of dormant perennials and dormant bulbous plants which are all good value for the five-minute gardener, provided you select plants that grow readily in your area.

Winter Annuals

Alyssum
Cineraria
Hollyhocks
Petite marigold
Polyanthus
Primula

Winter Perennials

Achillea
Perennial aster
Astilbe
Delphinium
Filipendula
Gerbera
Liatris
Michaelmas daisy
Russell lupin

Winter Bulbs

Agapanthus
Bearded iris
Calla
Canna
Dutch iris
Eucomis (pineapple lily)
Gladiolus
Hippeastrum
Ifafa lily
Japanese iris
Lilium
Lily-of-the-valley
Tigridia
Tuberose

A Winter Hot Spot

If you live in warmer areas, you won't be able to enjoy the elegant blooms of autumn crocus or the weird appeal of the fritillary family that grace the gardens of cooler areas. But with some careful autumn planning you'll have a hot spot in which to enjoy the morning winter sun, which never seems to warm up those cooler gardens. This potted scheme uses quick-growing annuals in brash golds to warm up cool days. All of these plants flower approximately three months after sowing, with the Californian poppies even faster than that. Autumn planting should see you with a fire-blaze of color through winter. Nasturtiums tumble from a hanging basket. Yellow cosmos climb out of a sea of white candytuft in a large pot at its feet, smaller pots of Californian poppies are the clear bright orange of egg yolks. Apart from those shown, pansies, zinnias, marigolds, and cleome will also flower nine weeks from sowing.

Keep plants watered, but be restrained with the liquid fertilizer until flowering starts. Over-fertilizing will cause leave growth at the expense of flowers.

Spring Plantings

Plant now for weeks, or even months, of summer color, if there's any room in your garden among the brilliant show that celebrates spring. Some attention to planting now will give you fresh color in the last hot months of summer when gardens are starting to look shabby.

Spring Annuals

Ageratum
Alyssum
Amaranthus
Aster
Balsam
Carnation
Celosia
Chrysanthemum
Cleome
Cosmos
Globe amaranth
Hollyhock
Marigold
Mexican poppy
Mignonette
Nasturtium
Painted daisy
Penstemon
Petunia
Phlox
Rudbeckia
Salpiglossis
Salvia
Snapdragon
Snow-on-the mountain
Statice
Strawflower
Swan River daisy
Verbena
Viscaria
Zinnia

Spring Bulbs

Canna
Crinum
Dahlia
Eucharis
Eucomis
Gladiolus
Gloriosa lily
Iris
Lycoris
Nerine
Sprekelia
Valotta
Zephyranthes

Summer Plantings

Among the spring-flowering annuals are some that will give autumn and winter flowers if planted from mid-summer to autumn. They can be sown from seed, or bought in seedling form in pots that become available around mid-August. This is just the time that the five-minute gardener may need some replacements to fill spaces left by spent plants.

Summer Annuals

Ageratum	Clarkia	Petunia
Alyssum	Cleome	Phlox
Antirrhinum	Globe amaranth	Pinks
Aster	Linaria	Rudbeckia
Calceolaria	Lobelia	Sweet William
Calendula	Marigold	Torenia
Candytuft	Nasturtium	Verbena
Carnation	Nepeta	Zinnia

Summer Perennials

Daisy	Gazania	Gerbera
Echium	Geranium	Stokesia

Summer Bulbs

Agapanthus	Daylily	Liriope
Canna	Dietes	Tulbaghia

A Year in the Five-Minute Flower Garden

Spring

The five-minute flower garden is pretty as a picture in spring as the bulbs celebrate the change of season and the spring-flowering annuals launch their colorful parade to summer. If you planned and planted well during autumn and early winter you'll be enjoying the delights of cineraria, pansy, poppy, and primula. Gardeners in warm climates will be impressed by poor man's orchid, everlasting daisy, sweet pea, and petunia.

Pests

With the triumph of new spring growth come aphids, never far behind those juicy green sprouts. Spray annuals and roses with pyrethrum to keep control of large numbers; rub individual invaders off with your fingers. Sugar scarab beetles may also be on the attack, particularly on white flowers. Spray with malathion. White or pale-colored flowers can also be attacked at this time of year by thrips. They prefer dry conditions, so watering over the flowers in the afternoon will offer some protection. A systemic spray will do the job completely, but so will the much safer option of a good downpour. Thrips are worst in a dry spring following a wet autumn. Be prepared.

Water

Windy spring weather can dry soil out fast, so you'll need to keep a watch on your watering schedule. In warm climates, keep the water up to annuals for a continuing good display.

Feeding

A weekly watering with a foliar fertilizer will keep plants growing strongly. Remove spent flower heads on annuals to keep them flowering; allowing them to set seed will soon see them dying off. Also dead-head early-blooming bulbs. This won't make them produce any more flowers but will stop then from wasting their energy on producing unwanted seed.

Weeding

Weeds grow quickly in warming soils. Keep them under control by scuffing around plants lightly with a hand fork. Cover ban spots with mulch and paint perennial weeds, such as onion weed, oxalis, and dandelion with a natural herbicide.

Summer

The summer garden is ablaze with annuals reveling in the hot weather. Alyssum, aster, bachelor's button, cosmos, daisies, petunia, phlox, verbena, and zinnia are all reliable summer stars.

In areas where there are water restrictions, maintain a good layer of mulch over the soil to help retain soil moisture. Water soil with a surfactant to improve its water-holding capacity.

Pests

Aphids are still feasting on new growth, while summer sees caterpillars getting into the act as well. Pyrethrum does away with the first, while the latter is best dealt with by dusting susceptible plants with Derris Dust or spraying with *Bacillus thuringiensis* (Dipel). Thrips might also be a problem and so might grasshoppers. Serious infestations of these chewers can be dealt with by malathion. Snail bait needs to be laid for snails throughout summer.

Watering

Turn on the watering system or the hose whenever the soil is dry to the touch. Early morning is the best time to water so that plants and soil have a chance to dry out during the day, discouraging fungal diseases. For the same reason, avoid watering over flowers. Daily watering may be necessary in hot dry weather, and of course, newly planted seedlings will need more frequent watering than established plants.

Feeding

Weekly watering with foliar fertilizer, such as Nitrosol, when plants reach bud stage will keep them growing strongly.

Weeding

Mulch around plants with dry lawn clippings, mulch from a mulcher or leaf litter to keep weeds down. If you need to weed, cover the bare spots with a handful of mulch so that more weeds don't spring up in the cleared space you have provided.

Autumn

The summer annuals come to an end in early autumn but marigolds, torenia, and of course roses, will continue to provide plenty of flowers and a bright display well into autumn. The main color display in the autumn garden, though,

comes from perennials such as chrysanthemum, dahlia, Easter or Michaelmas daisy (perennial aster), lobelia, penstemon, physostegia, helianthus, and the lovely Japanese wind anemone.

If you are growing plants in containers and watering with a watering can, use luke warm water (about the temperature of a baby's bath). This prevents the shock of chilling and your plants will grow better.

Pests

Aphids continue to attack new growth, especially on roses. Spray with pyrethrum. Several of the caterpillars also come out in big numbers during autumn. Control them with *Bacillus thuringiensis* (Dipel). Watch snails on new plantings of bulbs and seedlings and use snail bait to keep them at bay. Snail spray can be used on tall plants.

Watering

Water only if soil is dry, though germinating seeds and newly planted seedlings will need more regular attention. Morning watering will help avoid fungal disease.

Feeding

Reduce feeding on established plants and lawns; but a half-strength foliar fertilizer will keep seedlings moving.

Weeding

Hand weed carefully around emerging bulbs and young annuals. The weeds will take the sun, water, and fertilizer from your growing plants. Mulch over any bare spots to prevent a second generation of weed invaders.

Frost Care

Frost-tender plants, such as cinerarias, will need covering on frosty nights. Rows can be protected with plastic tunnels or individual plants can be covered with cloche made by cutting the base out of a plastic container such as an orange juice bottle. The covers should be taken off during the day and replaced each evening. Just leave them beside the plants or rows for quick replacement. Plants will stay warmer and be less vulnerable to frosts if they are also well mulched with spoiled alfalfa hay, straw, or autumn leaves run between the rows and tucked around each plant. The mulch will also keep weeds down. Put a few snail bait granules around to combat any snails and slugs that hide in the mulch.

The frost protection routine will use up at least two of your five minutes morning and evening, leaving you not much time to check for snails and leaf miner which both attack cinerarias, or to turn on the watering system. The five-minute gardener won't have time to pamper too many frost-tender plants. Skip if they prove too time-consuming.

Winter

The winter garden need not be flower-free. Of the annuals, ageratum will throw up its blue puffball flowers through the cold months, while Iceland poppy, pansy, polyanthus, primula, and violet can all be coaxed to flower if planted early enough.

The early-flowering bulbs such as early jonquils and daffodils and snowflakes also brighten the winter garden. Of the perennials, hellebores will produce a mass of flowers in delicate shades of pale green, through to robust dark purples. They even make great cut flowers. Of the shrubs, Reinwardtia is a showy performer with primrose yellow flowers in mild to warm districts.

Pests

Pests are not much of a problem during the colder winter months but watch out for slugs and snails—scatter a little snail bait around seedlings and emerging bulbs. Aphids can infest new growth on annuals. Pansies with flower petals that are rolled up will be infested with aphids. Gently unroll petals and brush aphids away if you only have a few showing these signs, or spray with pyrethrum if the problem seems bad. Cinerarias may be attacked by caterpillars—spray with *Bacillus thuringiensis* (Dipel). They are also prone to leaf miner as are

nasturtiums and marguerite daisies. Leaves show typical white, wavy lines—spray with malathion.

Watering

Don't neglect watering just because it is cold. Soils will dry out rapidly in windy weather whatever the temperature. Water only if the soil is dry and water in the morning so that the soil has a chance to warm up during the day. Plants left in cold, wet soil do not thrive. Do not water if the soil is wet unless you have to water plants in the very early morning to counteract the effect of frosts.

Feeding

Growth slows down when the soil is cold in winter and plants are not using a lot of fertilizer, so feeding should be restricted to plants that are actively growing, such as spring-flowering bulbs, annuals, and perennials. These can be given a fortnightly watering with one of the foliar fertilizers, such as Nitrosol, when buds start to form.

Weeding

Keep the garden weeded carefully while seedlings and bulbs are growing. It's a funny thing that weeds grow just as rapidly winter or summer while your plants grow very slowly in cold weather. This means the weeds can easily smother them. Cover the bare soil with a handful of leaf mulch (there should be plenty around if you have deciduous trees). This will suppress fresh germinations and save a second weeding.

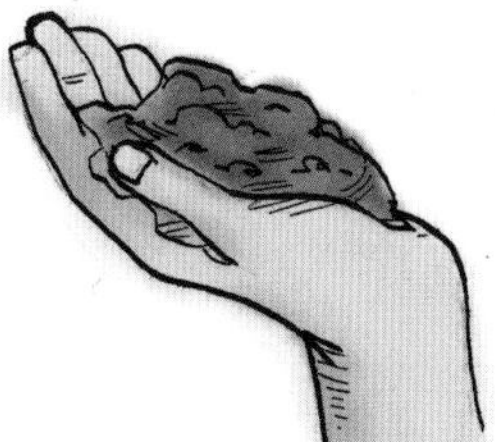

Flower Selections

Flower Selections

Success in the five-minute flower garden is assured if you pick the right flowers. Almost everything is easy to grow given the right conditions. In places where summers are dry and hot and winters are cool and wet, for example, stocks grow like weeds, self-seeding as freely as forget-me-nots do in other climates. Most gardeners can't resist trying to grow things that don't really fit their climate, but the best results will come from the local reliables. Here are some flowers to choose from, none of them so fragile or rare that the five-minute gardener should have any trouble procuring or growing them.

Key
* Very easy to grow

** Easy to grow given the right conditions

*** Might require some attention but worth the effort

Ageratum *

These dwarf border plants give a good display through most of the year. Ageratum is usually blue but there are also some unusual pink, white, and bi-colors available as bedding plants. Ageratum grows best in full sun but is also suitable for semi-shade. Sow in all but cold weather either direct into beds or in seed boxes. Thin or transplant to 6–8 inches (15–20cm) apart. Once established plants need little care other than watering in hot weather. Liquid feeds will encourage flowering.

Varieties: Blue Mink, Blue Blazer, Blue Tango, Blue Blanket (new and recommended), Pinkie, White Cushion, Harlequin Mix

Tip: Shear to remove spent flowers and encourage a fresh flush.

Alyssum *

Excellent edging, carpeting, and rockery plant, alyssum flowers year-round in most climates. The sweet fragrance of the tiny flowers gives it a popular name of sweet Alice and it is available in white, pink, lilac, and violet. Alyssum loves a hot, dry position but will tolerate some shade. Grow it from seed sown in clumps, or as bedding plants 3–4 inches (7–10cm) apart.

Varieties: Carpet of Snow (best for paving), Cameo Mixture, Royal Carpet, Peaches & Cream

Tip: Alyssum is great in sandy soils and seaside gardens and is a good choice for cushion planting in cracks in paths and paved areas.

Amaranthus **

A tall (at least 3 feet/1m) summer annual grown for its brilliant foliage color. Sow it in spring where it is to grow and thin to 18 inches (45cm). Cover seed with vermiculite and keep damp until seedlings appear. Thin to 16 inches (40cm) and plant thinnings after discarding pale-colored plants. Liquid feeds will encourage good leaf growth and color. Amaranthus loves hot, dry summers as long as it is given regular watering.

Varieties: Flying Colors, Flaming Fountain

Tip: Keep snail bait around and watch for caterpillars—pick off or spray with *Bacillus thuringiensis* (Dipel). Both of these pests will damage foliage and spoil the display.

Aster **

Asters are good cut flowers for summer and should be grown in a sunny, open bed with friable soil and good drainage. Sow seed from spring to summer in seed boxes. Alternatively buy pots of beddings plants and transplant 8 inches

(20cm) apart into beds that have been prepared with complete fertilizer and compost. A mulch over the surface in summer will keep roots cool. Avoid watering over plants as this may encourage mildew, which may be a problem in humid weather.

Tip: Asters are most suited to light or sandy soils and are not recommended for the five-minute gardener with heavy clay soils where Aster Wilt may be a problem.

Balsam *

This is one of the impatiens but if differs from the popular busy Lizzie in that it will grow in full sun, while still tolerating part shade. The flowers are double, downward-facing and are pink, white, and rose shades. Raise balsam from seed in pots or direct sow when the weather warms. Plant out 12 inches (30cm) apart. Plants grow to about 20 inches (50cm) and flowers appear about eight weeks from sowing. Prepare soil before planting with compost and a ration of complete fertilizer and water well in hot, dry weather.

Tip: Balsam is a good choice for window boxes or raised troughs and pots with morning sun where the down-facing flowers can be shown to advantage.

Begonia **

Bedding or wax begonia is a useful plant for the five-minute gardener as it flowers freely over many months and its neat, dwarf form makes it an ideal edging or dwarf hedge plant much used in formal plantings. Buy advanced plants or raise from seed, which is very fine and should be covered lightly with vermiculite and kept damp until germination. Plant out seedlings 8 inches (20cm) apart, water regularly until established and give regular feeds of foliar fertilizer. Flower colors include white, pinks, and reds and some varieties have colorful foliage. Grow in full sun, part-shade in hot districts.

Tip: Wax begonias are perennials but may be grown as annuals in very hot or very cold winter districts. Shear over when flowers finish for fresh growth and further flowering.

Bellis Perennis *

Sow English Daisy seed in autumn or plant out advanced bedding plants. English daisies will grow in full sun or part shade and with their delicate pink and white daisy flowers, make good edging plants. They grow readily in soil that has a good ration of humus and some complete fertilizer added. Keep plants watered while they are growing and give liquid feeds once flower buds form. New varieties have larger flowers on longer stems and are better for picking. Separate colors of red, pink, white, or pink-and-white are now available.

Tip: English daisy is a lawn daisy. If you have a rather damp, shady lawn that is not growing well, oversow it with daisy seeds.

Calendula *

Also known as the English or pot marigold, these cheerful flowers are good for cutting and very easy to raise from seed sown in spring or autumn (popular for winter flowers). They do well in any soil but grow best in well-prepared and composted sunny beds and flower within 10 weeks of sowing. Colors range from all shades of yellow to orange and gold, even cream and white, and some flowers are double. Rust may be a problem in humid weather. Remove and put into the bin any badly infected plants and spray the rest with fungicide. Deadhead spent blooms to keep the flowers coming.

Tip: Plant in full sun with good air circulation for healthy plants. This is the plant referred to as pot marigold in recipes for cooking or herbal ointment. The petals are used in salads.

Californian Poppy *

This native of California and similar areas in the US will carpet the sunny garden with brilliant poppy-like blooms held above gray-green fine-cut foliage. They are hard to transplant so are best sown where they are to grow. Once established they will self-sow. Modern varieties add a range of pinks, white, and reds, single or double, to the original yellow and gold. Not suitable for picking, they give a great display of color in the garden.

Tip: Californian poppy is a good choice for a hot, dry summer climate similar to their native California.

Candytuft **

There are two types of candytuft; "hyacinth-flowered", which is white and flowers up the stem, and "umbellata", which has flowers at the top of the stem. Both grow readily from seed sown where it is to grow and are not fussy about soil as long as drainage is good. Grow candytuft in full sun (though it will tolerate some shade). Sow in autumn (spring in cold winter areas) in beds prepared with compost and a dressing of complete fertilizer. Sow direct or transplant 8 inches (20cm) apart. Give liquid feeds when plants start flowering.

Tip: Candytuft is good for cutting and Iceberg gives a strong highlight planted with anemone and ranunculus.

Canterbury Bells **

Add spires to the flower garden with these 3 feet (1m) tall stems of cup-and-saucer flowers—wonderful for flower arrangements and a beautiful color range from white to delicate pink, rose, blue, and mauve. Canterbury bells are easiest planted out from pots of advanced seedlings in autumn, in to well-composted soil at 12-inch (30cm) spacing.

Tip: Plant in a sunny position, sheltered from strong wind if you want to use the flower in flower arrangements as in part shade the stems will bend out towards the sun, spoiling them for arranging.

Carnation ***

This is a great addition to the five-minute flower garden because of its fragrance. Plant spring or autumn from cuttings or bedding plants available in pots (germination from seed is slow and erratic). Carnations need sun and first-class drainage and an open, uncrowded position; they do well in raised beds. Add plenty of organic matter to heavy soils and also to light, sandy soils, plus a pre-planting fertilizer. Carnations like a slightly alkaline soil so add a dressing of lime—1 tablespoon per square foot (half a cup per square meter) on sandy soils, but 1½ tablespoons per square foot (1 cup per square meter) on heavy soils. Leave for a couple of weeks before planting. Space plants 12–16 inches (30–40cm) apart. Pinch plants back when about 6 inches (15cm) tall to induce side shoots. Repeat pinching when side shoots reach 6 inches (15cm). Best grown as an annual in humid climates, carnations can be cut back to reflower in temperate zones.

Tip: In humid areas grow carnations in a wire "collar" to hold plants up away from soil where they will rot.

Celosia *

This is quick and easy to grow from seed sown in spring or early summer. Sow direct or plant out from pots. Thin or transplant to 8–12 inches (20–30cm) apart. Water regularly and mulch to keep weeds down. There are tall dwarf varieties with plumes of gold, yellow, pink, salmon, or crimson.

Tip: Celosia is a good choice for hot summer climates. It loves heat but must be kept watered and fed with liquid fertilizer when flowering starts.

Chrysanthemum **

Perennial chrysanthemums are good cut flowers for the picking garden. Shasta daisy gives masses of white summer flowers while the popular "mums" are great for cutting in autumn. Grow from cuttings or rooted sections taken in spring or early summer. The annual chrysanthemum, painted daisy, gives a good display through summer, growing 24–30 inches (60–75cm) with white flowers brightly zoned red, yellow, and purple. They are also good for cutting. The small, white-flowered star daisy is another chrysanthemum that can be used as an edging plant.

Tip: Stake perennial chrysanthemums and tie flowering stems as they grow, otherwise they bow down in rain and get muddy, stems become bent and unsuitable for using as cut flowers.

Cineraria **

These are wonderful for semi-shade and make showy pot plants (in 8-inch/20cm pots), which can be moved indoors when flowering starts. A rich color range is available in both dwarf and tall varieties. Cineraria is easily raised from seed sown in late summer and will self-sow in temperate climates. For the five-minute gardener they are easiest to grow from advanced bedding plants in pots, available in autumn and winter and, for the balcony flower gardener they are available in late winter and spring in flower in containers. Plant out 12 inches (30cm) apart into well-drained, well-composted soil with a dressing of complete fertilizer mixed through and watered in. Problems include snails and caterpillars which damage leaves—use snail pellets; and aphids on flower buds—spray with pyrethrum.

Tip: Cineraria is frost-tender so in frosty districts grow in glass or a shade house or cover on frosty nights.

Cleome **

Often called spider flower because of its mass of arching stamens, cleome is a tall (3–10 feet/1–2m), handsome annual for the back of the border, a good cut flower and long blooming in the garden. Sow seed in clumps 20 inches (50cm) apart direct where it is to grow, in spring or early summer or early autumn. Flowers are pink, lilac, mauve, or white and foliage is large and maple-like. Cleome needs good drainage and full sun for at least part of the day and does well on any average garden soil.

Tip: Plant cleome in a position where it is sheltered from strong winds and protect from snails and caterpillars, which are attracted to the leaves.

Columbine *

Also called Aquilegia or granny's bonnets because of the shape of the flowers, these are readily raised from seed sown where it is to grow or in seed boxes in late summer or autumn (in spring also in cold districts). Columbines are also often available in pots now that cottage garden plants are so popular. Plant out 12 inches (30cm) apart and keep watered. A mulch of composted lawn clippings or leaf mold around them will keep down weeds. Soluble fertilizer should be given when buds start to form. As columbines are perennials they may flower poorly in the first year but will do better in the second season. They suit a cool, moist position in sun or filtered or part shade and should be replanted every second year in warmer areas.

Tip: The maidenhair-like foliage of columbines is a pretty bonus. Old-fashioned types look wonderful in a cottage garden.

Cornflower **

Traditionally blue, this charming cottage flower is now available in pinks, rose, maroon, lavender, and white. It grows well in morning sun and needs well-drained soil with a dressing of lime added. Sow seed in seedling boxes through autumn or plant out from pots of advanced bedding plants. Space 16 inches (40cm) apart and give soluble fertilizer feeds every two weeks when buds develop. Plants grow up to 24 inches (60cm) and are good cut flowers.

Tip: Cornflowers were one of the field flowers that grew with red poppies and white daisies in the cornfields. Try a "field-flower" planting of these three flowers using cornflower mystic blue, Flanders poppy, and white star daisies—great for a cottage or country garden.

Cosmos *

Cosmos is a great choice for the five-minute gardener as it can be grown rapidly from seed sown where it is to grow in spring and summer. Plants are tall (over 3 feet/1m) with ferny leaves and masses of large daisy flowers in white, pinks, crimsons, and mauve tones, which are good for picking. They are sometimes available in pots as cottage plants, particularly a white variety. There are also species with yellows, orange, red and mahogany shades, which are smaller and more compact, with double or single flowers.

Tip: Plant tall-growing cosmos in clumps where they can support one another. Pick a position sheltered from strong wind. Watch for sensational new chocolate cosmos—chocolate-colored and perfumed.

Dahlia **

Dahlias can be grown from tubers, seed or seedlings and are good value for the five-minute gardener as they flower over a long period through summer and autumn, until the first frost kills them off. Give them a sunny position in well-drained soil with plenty of compost and manures, particularly in sandy soils. Add a light dressing of lime if soil is acid. Sow seed in spring or early summer (for autumn blooms). Tubers are planted during spring and are lifted in December for replanting next season. As plants grow, give a dressing of complete fertilizer or blood and bone—1¾ ounces (50g) per plant. Liquid feeds should be started when buds appear. Dahlias come in a wide range of types such as decorative, cactus, charm, collarette, water lily, and pompone. The dwarf varieties are sold in pots and make colorful edgings. The tree dahlia, *D. imperialis*, is an interesting species that has light mauve flowers in late autumn and into winter.

Tip: If you can spare the space, the five-minute gardener can save time and work with dahlias by leaving the clumps of tubers in position. Simply cut back in December and cover with a layer of leaf mulch through winter.

Delphinium ***

Delphinium is a splendid plant that can be grown as an annual in warmer and temperate areas or as a perennial in cold districts. Prepare the bed well with organic matter and a dressing of complete fertilizer. Add a light dressing of lime in acid soils. Buy advanced bedding plants in autumn or early spring and plant out 20 inches (50cm) apart into soil that has been watered the evening before so that it is "damp dark." Mulch around the plants through summer and feed once every two weeks with liquid fertilizer once plants are growing. Colors range from white through blues to purple, pink, and lavender. There are also red species, *D. Cardinale* and *D. nudicaule*.

Tip: Stake tall varieties at planting time and plant in a position sheltered from strong winds.

Dianthus **

Dianthus belongs to the carnation family but is easier to grow in many areas. Grow in very well-drained soil and don't water if the soil is still damp from a previous watering. Colors range from reds and crimsons through to mauves and pinks and white, often in striking combination. Grow Dianthus from seed in spring or autumn or buy advanced plants in pots. They are often offered in bloom in mini-pots. Dianthus can be grown as an annual, but in all but the very hottest districts, it can be cut back after flowering, fed and it will continue to bloom. Dianthus suits garden beds, borders, pots, and troughs. It is good for picking and many varieties are fragrant.

Tip: Put Dianthus in the sunniest best-drained position you have for the best results.

Evening Primrose *

The tall yellow evening primrose flowers for months with fresh flowers opening each evening, but for the five-minute gardener, a better choice is the pink evening primrose, *Oenothera speciosa*. The masses of delicate pink flowers stay open all day and the plants are low-growing and drought-tolerant, making a neat border in full sun. Sow from seed in autumn or spring, or from rooted divisions in spring.

Tip: Plant the night-flowering evening primrose if you suffer from insomnia or rise very early—they look wonderful by moonlight and at dawn.

Everlasting Daisy *

Paper daisy and *Helichrysum bracteatum* (straw flower) are native Australian daisies with papery petals that dry well. They tolerate most soils as long as they get full sun. Sow seed in autumn or spring in clumps where they are to grow. Straw flower can also be raised in pots or seedling boxes and planted out when around 3 inches (7cm) in clumps, or 12 inches (30cm) apart. Straw flower comes in white, pink, red, gold, and mauve and grows to 30 inches (75cm). Paper daisies come in white, pink, and red. Don't dig around these plants, as they don't appreciate root disturbance. Give a little liquid fertilizer when buds appear.

Tip: To dry, cut flowers as soon as they open and hang upside down in loose bunches in a dry, airy place until the stems are dry.

Forget-Me-Not *

The perfect choice for the partly shaded garden, forget-me-not thrives moist, shady spots and can be grown as an edging around garden beds or as a ground cover under trees. Though the usual forget-me-not is blue with a yellow eye there are white and pink forms available too. Grow in autumn from seed sown where it is to grow or in pots to be transplanted 12 inches (30cm) apart when plants are big enough to handle. Seed is slow to germinate (up to 21 or 28 days) and must be kept damp during this time.

Tip: When they start to seed, pull out plants or shear over to remove the spent flowering heads with the clinging seeds that tangle with clothing. Where it is used as a ground cover, shear over lightly. This will produce a second flowering.

Gazania **

This South African daisy is a good choice for the five-minute gardener with a hot, dry, sunny bank, driveway, or rockery. Once planted you should have this neat little perennial daisy forever. It forms a tidy mat, ideal for dwarf edgings along your driveway for instance and flowers freely all through the warm months with cream, yellow, pink, mahogany, white, or bicolored daisies. Plant from divisions or sow seeds in pots in spring or summer and transplant when 2–8-inch (5–20cm) spacings. Look for new varieties with dramatic colors and large, colorful single or double flowers at nurseries.

Tip: Gazanias are great for holding soil on sandy banks and for seaside plantings. It will form a silvery gray-green carpet year-round with flowers through warm, sunny weather.

Gerbera **

Another South African daisy that thrives in a hot, sunny climate, Gerberas are a great choice for the five-minute gardener in a warm climate where it flowers year-round. Gerbera is also a good source of cut flowers. It is easy to raise from seed sown in pots or seedling boxes in spring or early summer (cover seed with vermiculite) or grow from rooted divisions taken year-round (winter is a popular time) in warm to tropical areas (autumn in temperate zones). Good drainage is vital and an open, sandy soil is best. Prepare soil with a ration of complete fertilizer and a dressing of lime if soil is acid.

Tip: When planting keep crown of plant above the soil to avoid rotting. Replant every three years.

Godetia **

These pretty annuals are called "Farewell to Spring" because they flower when most other spring annuals have finished—a good addition to the five-minutes flower garden to keep up that flowery look with combinations of pink, crimson, lilac, and white. Seed can be sown in autumn (or early spring in cold areas) and can be scattered where it is to grow among the plants. Thin seedlings if they are too close together. Don't overfeed godetias or they will be all leaf—a pre-planting fertilizer and watering when dry is sufficient.

Globe Amaranth *

Also called Gomphrena this is an easily grown, summer-flowering plant that has purple, clover-like flowers on a plant growing around 12 inches (30cm). It is long-flowering and particularly good in hot, dry summer climates. It is also a good choice for the balcony gardener in a hot area. Plants grow readily from seed sown direct where they are to grow in spring or early summer and are available in pots from nurseries. Encourage flowering by foliar feeding every two weeks after buds appear.

Tip: Gomphrena can be dried for flower arrangements. Pick and hang upside down in loose bunches so that stems dry straight in a cool, dry place.

Hollyhock **

Hollyhock is a favorite for the cottage garden in temperate and cool gardens. Plants grow 7–10 feet (2–3m) and should be in full sun, sheltered from wind. Stake plants in windy areas. Hollyhocks will grow in any garden soil with the addition of compost and a complete fertilizer before planting. Sow in late summer or early autumn in seedling boxes or pots (cover lightly with vermiculite) so that they will flower in the first year. Transplant 12 inches (30cm) apart and do not crowd them with too much other growth. They are susceptible to rust and crowding will increase the humidity. Spray with fungicide if rust is noticed. When 12 inches (30cm) high, give side-dressings of a foliar fertilizer. Flowers may be single or double in white, pink, red, and yellow.

Tip: Hollyhocks are very attractive to slugs and snails—keep up snail bait and check under leaves and remove snails frequently.

Impatiens *

Also known as busy Lizzie, this is a wonderful plant for the five-minute gardener as it can flower for at least nine months of the year (longer in warm areas). Modern hybrid and dwarf forms are much better plants than the old forms. Most varieties have single flowers but some rose-like doubles are available. All are great for shady gardens and moist soils but modern forms will do equally well in sunny gardens. Busy Lizzie is easy to grow from cuttings. It can also be easily raised from seed sown in spring or summer in seedling boxes or pots, and planted out or potted on when 3 inches (7cm) high. New Guinea impatiens has colorful foliage and very large flowers and needs good morning sun to flower well and develop good leaf color. Water regularly in hot or dry weather. This is a great choice for the balcony or patio gardener but is frost tender and should be protected or moved indoors as pot plants in winter in cold, frosty areas. Prune back when flower flush finished to keep compact.

Tip: The only pest of impatiens is the caterpillar of the impatiens hawkmoth—a huge but attractive black caterpillar which can defoliate plants overnight. Pick off and spray plants with *Bacillus thuringiensis* (Dipel) if attacked.

Larkspur **

These charming, tall annuals grow up to 24 inches (60cm) or more, which makes them good for cutting. They come in a range of pretty pinks, white, roses, light and dark blues and grow in most home garden conditions, responding well to well-drained, well-prepared soil and plenty of sunshine. Sow seeds in autumn in clumps where they are to grow. Soil should be damp-dark and seed covered with vermiculite. Alternatively, buy advanced bedding plants in pots and plant in groups of two or three so that they will support each other. Give liquid feed every two weeks as buds appear and keep watered in dry or windy weather.

Tip: Larkspurs are similar to delphiniums but are easier to grow in warm climates.

Linaria *

Often called eggs and bacon by gardeners, these flowers look like mini-snapdragons, growing about 12 inches (30cm) high, and are easily and quickly grown in any garden soil. Sow seed direct where it is to grow in rows or clumps among other plants from early autumn to early winter or spring in cold areas. Flowers appear within ten weeks of sowing in a range of pastel colors from cream and yellow through apricot, pink, and mauve.

Tip: Plants can be grown quite thickly without worrying about thinning to give a dense mass of color. Pick for posies. Shear off after flowering for a second flush.

Livingstone Daisy **

For an easy hit of brilliant color in winter and spring, you can't beat the little Livingstone daisy. Plants only grow to around 6 inches (15cm) and smother themselves with a really vivid blanket of multi-colored flowers in full sun. Grow them in rockeries, as a ground-covering border around taller plants or in troughs on a sunny balcony. Sow seed in autumn to early winter or buy pots of advanced bedding plants. Water until plants are established but then only in dry weather. They will grow anywhere and in any soil provided drainage is good.

Tip: Livingstone daisies must be planted in full sun as these flowers close in shade and in overcast or rainy weather.

Lobelia *

This is a great little plant for masses of flowers in window boxes, borders, edging, baskets, and rockeries. Blue varieties are bright and pure—among the best of blues for the garden. Sow seed in autumn or by seedlings in pots. Seed is fine so water seed raising mix before sowing and cover gently with vermiculite. Transplant to 1 inch (3cm) apart when big enough to handle. They will grow in full sun or partial shade with morning sun and flower over a long period in temperate climates.

Mixture (long flowering, good color range), Lavender Cascade, Electric Blue, Lilac Mist

Tip: Plant lobelia in containers or as a garden edging with yellow violas or petite marigold and white alyssum for a bright contrast.

Lupin *

Lupins are the answer to what to grow if you have fairly poor soil. In fact, they will flower better in soil that is not heavily fertilized. They are nitrogen-fixing plants and will actually improve the soil with no work from you. Add a light dressing of lime to the soil, plus a little complete fertilizer before planting. Dust seed with fungicide and sow in autumn where it is to grow in clumps of three or four seeds 12–16 inches (30–40cm) apart. If seed is sown into soil that is dark-damp (water the night before) you won't need to give too much water while seed is germinating. Bedding plants are also available in pots. Tall-growing varieties can be thinned to two plants and the extra seedlings transplanted. Flowers are pink, blue, mauve, yellow, and white and all are sweetly scented. When flowering starts, give an occasional feeding with half-strength liquid fertilizer to prolong flowering. Mulch around roots to keep cool.

Tip: The splendid Russell lupins should only be attempted in cool to cold climates. They are perennial and at their best for around five years.

Marigold *

Gardeners in frost-free gardens can have marigolds all year round by growing African marigolds through summer and planting the French marigolds in autumn. All marigolds need full sun and tolerate poor soils but will respond well to pre-planting additions of compost and complete fertilizer. They germinate readily from seed sown in spring and into mid-summer and can be sown where they are to grow or in seedling boxes. Marigolds are sold in pots and also in bloom in mini-pots at nurseries. The Petite marigolds make charming garden edgings and grow well in containers. The taller varieties grow up to 30 inches (75cm) and make a great autumn display when most other annuals are past their best. Protect plants from snails, which are very attracted to the aromatic foliage.

Tip: Marigolds are great companion plants and help get rid of nematodes in the soil.

Mimulus ***

This is an old favorite, known as monkey musk, which is popular again with new, improved varieties available. Grow from seed sown in spring in seedling boxes of seed raising mix and transplant into pots or the garden. Mimulus thrives in semi-shade and likes to be kept watered. Flowers are a mixture of reds, yellows, and pinks, and many are speckled and spotted with maroon or red.

Tip: Mimulus is suitable for shady balconies or partly shaded gardens, but is frost-tender.

Nasturtium *

One of the easiest of annuals to grow, nasturtiums are guaranteed to provide masses of flowers which can be picked and even eaten. Some will run all over the ground or climb, while others are compact but all grow rapidly from seed sown where it is to grown. Flowers are mainly single but there are double varieties and colors range from cream to yellow, orange and red, many of which are bi-colored. There is no need to enrich the soil as this will encourage leaf growth at the expense of flowers. Nasturtiums grow in sun or dappled sunlight. Grow trailing varieties over banks or walls—they are great cover-ups of waster spaces; use compact varieties in containers, baskets, and garden beds. If you have a particularly good color you can grow more plants by taking cuttings.

Tip: Use nasturtium buds, flowers and young leaves in salads. The seeds can be pickled and used as you would use capers.

Nemesia *

This is a plant for massed flower display in late winter and spring. Sow seed in autumn to early winter of plant seedlings. Seed can be sown direct into rows or in clumps. Plants flower from 14 weeks after sowing. Colors range from cream to lemon, yellow, gold, orange, scarlet, and red and plants will grow 8–12 inches (20–30cm) high. The lovely blue gem is a dwarf plant growing to around 8 inches (20cm) with sky blue flowers and makes a good edging or container plant. Keep watered (not over the flowers) and give liquid feeds every two weeks to keep up flowering.

Tip: For bushy plants, pinch out the leading stems.

Nemophila **

Baby blue eyes is a delightful pure blue annual with ferny foliage which grows to around 8–12 inches (20–30cm). Grow it from seed sown where it is to grow in garden beds in a warm, sunny spot. Sow in autumn (or spring in cold districts) in friable, well-drained garden soil. Feed every two weeks with foliar fertilizer once buds develop.

Tip: Baby blue eyes does not transplant well so must be sown where it is to grow. Try planting it among spring bulbs.

Nigella *

love-in-a-mist or devil-in-a-fog—both are popular names for this pretty annual which is so easy to grow from seed that once you plant it you will find it popping up again and again. Flowers are mostly blue, hiding shyly among the green ferny foliage. Pink and white varieties are also available and all have decorative seed pods. Sow seed in autumn where it is to grow or plant out from seedling boxes or pots. Plants grow to around 16 inches (40cm) and should be sheltered form strong winds.

Tip: Make successive sowings from early spring to summer for months of flowers. Excellent for cutting.

Pansy *

A great favorite for garden beds, edgings and containers, there are many varieties of pansy in a range of sizes and colors with attractive blotched "faces." They must have well-drained soil and at least six hours of sun a day. Prepare beds before planting with compost well-rotted manure and a light dressing of complete fertilizer, which should be dug through the soil, watered in and left for at least a week before planting. Seeds can be planted from mid-summer (later in humid districts) and seedlings are available from mid-August. Plant out 8 inches (20cm) apart and add a little mulch around plants to encourage good root development. Do not water over the flowers and give feeds of liquid fertilizer every two weeks once flowering starts.

Tip: Keep picking off dead heads for long flowering. Pick for posies and low bowls.

Petunia **

One of the top-selling annuals, Petunias are a great standby for summer flowers. Grow from seed or advanced bedding plants available in a wide range of varieties. Plant in spring (or autumn in warm, frost-free areas). Seed is very fine so water seed raising mix first, mix seed with fine, dry, clean sand, then sprinkle over using a container with a shaker top, such as a spice bottle. Keep in a warm, sheltered place until germinated. Plant in full sun in garden beds, troughs, or hanging baskets. Petunias are good around pools and entertaining areas.

Tip: Water around root area only, not over the flowers as this spreads gray mold fungus. Petunias are very tolerant of dry conditions. Try a new type of perennial petunia, which has recently become available. It can be pruned off to grow again or can simply be grown as an annual. It is very free-flowering and tough.

Phlox **

Along with petunias, phlox is one of the best annuals for summer color and a sweet scent. For the five-minute gardener, dwarf phlox, growing to around 8 inches (20cm), will provide a flowery border which thrives in full or almost-full sun in well-drained soil. The phlox color range is wide and many have the traditional white eye while some have starry petals. Seed can be sown direct where it is to grow into soil prepared with compost or rotted manure and a dressing of complete fertilizer. Advanced plants are available in pots. Do not overwater phlox once they are growing strongly, however, the roots are shallow and a light mulch of dried lawn clipping around the root area will protect them from drying out.

Tip: Do not water over the flowers when phlox start to bloom. Water over the root area only to prevent fungal disease.

Polynathus ***

Though a perennial plant, polyanthus primrose is often grown as an annual, particularly in warm-temperate areas. In cool climates it is usually grown as a perennial. It is a very popular plant for spring and flowers over a long period in the garden or in containers. Polyanthus are valuable for the partly shady garden but will also tolerate sunnier positions. Give them well-drained soil and regular feeds of a foliar fertilizer to keep them flowering. The five-minute gardener will probably prefer to buy them in mini-pots (available through autumn, winter, and early spring) already in bloom for planting into garden borders or pots on a part-shady balcony. Colors range from primrose to cream, pink, blue, mauve, crimson, and red with contrasting eyes. Plants with flowers growing on single stems are the true primrose while a multi-flowered head on a single stem is a polyanthus.

Tip: Polyanthus plants often exhaust themselves with flowering and are best treated as an annual in warm, coastal gardens. In colder areas give them summer shade and mulch over heavily in summer with compost and manure.

Poppy **

Iceland poppies are a must for the picking garden—they make wonderful cut flowers, unlike other poppies (Shirley, Flander), which fall quickly. For good results prepare the soil well in advance with compost, manure, and complete fertilizer. Give poppies excellent drainage, full sun and shelter from strong winds. Start sowing seed in late summer for winter flowers. In warm climates sow or plant from autumn to early winter. Transplant seedlings 8–12 inches (20–30cm) apart and handle carefully as they are fragile. Do not cultivate around them as this damages the roots and weakens the plants—hand weed and mulch to keep weeds down. When buds start, give feed of foliar fertilizer every two weeks.

Tip: Pinch out early buds until the plants have developed into good clumps. For cut flowers, cut in bud and scald ends of stems before arranging.

Portulaca *

This is a great, low-growing border plant for the five-minute gardener as it grows readily, is pest and disease-free and flowers freely in a range of clear pastel colors. Sow direct in spring or plant out from advanced bedding plants in early summer. Plants must have good drainage and full sun to do well and don't mind dry conditions. Grow them in containers—troughs, window-boxes or hanging baskets—on a hot sunny balcony.

Tip: Most portulaca closes on overcast days which is frustrating in a wet summer. New varieties, however, such as cocktail and sun jewels, are able to stay open on dull days and are very rewarding.

Primula *

One of the best annuals for winter/ spring flowers, primula flowers well in partial shade. Colors range from white, pinks, and, mauve to crimson and ruby red. They are long-flowering and need little care other than watering once established. Add anything old and organic to the soil before planting—manures, compost, and if soil is acid, give a light dressing of lime

(1½ tablespoons per square foot/1 cup per square meter). Primula will grow readily from seed sown where it is to grow and is also a great self-seeder. Seed is very fine and can be sprinkled over the soil and pressed down or covered lightly with vermiculite. A wide range of varieties is available in bedding plants. Good for edgings (or double edging with lower-growing ageratum in front); among bulbs; in containers for a part shady balcony or patio and can be brought indoors when it begins to flower.

Tip: Some people are allergic to the foliage of primulas and will develop a contact dermatitis if exposed. Take care when handling if you have other contact allergies.

Salpiglossis ***

This is something different for the five-minute flower gardener. It must be grown from seed sown where it is to grow as it does not transplant. Salpiglossis is a tall plant with trumpet flowers unusually marked and veined in interesting shades of bronze, gold, red, and violet. Prepare soil well with organic matter and some complete fertilizer and sow in spring or early summer (spring in warmer areas) in a warm, sunny spot. Cover seed with vermiculite and keep damp until seedlings emerge (up to 21 days). Plants flower within 12 weeks from sowing and should be kept watered in hot weather.

Tip: Plants are tall and brittle—plant out of the wind and in clumps so that they will support one another.

Salvia *

Salvias give the five-minute gardener a wonderful return for space and time. They flower freely over a long period—all through the warm months—are drought and heat resistant and are rarely troubled by any pests or diseases. They are perennial plants but are usually grown as annuals. If pruned after flowering, they will repeat flower and can last for two years or more. They do best in full sun but the shrubby bonfire-type salvias will also grow and flower in partial shade. The old scarlet *S. Splendens* has been joined by modern strains, which are more compact and available in a range of colors from red to maroon, crimson, mauve, pink, and white. Salvia makes a stunning border planting (up to 24 inches/ 60cm tall) in mixed colors. Blue and white forms of *S. fariniacea* can be grown the same way and also have long-lasting flower spikes. Grow all salvia from seed sown in autumn (spring in cold districts) or bedding plants in spring. For the five-minute gardener advanced plants, either in pots or mini-pots already in bloom, will save time and energy.

Tip: Blue and white salvia is a good substitute for lavender in a cottage garden in humid coastal areas where lavender doesn't do well.

Saponaria **

Better known as big gyp, this is as easy to grow from seed as its namesake, gypsophila (gyp to the florists) but is a soft pink color. Big Gyp can be sown at any time of the year (avoiding excessively hot, cold, or wet periods). Sow where it is to grow—this plant makes a good display in a mass planting so don't bother to thin seedlings. Flowers appear within eight weeks after sowing and are excellent for cutting.

Tip: Saponaria is excellent for the picking garden—make successive sowings every few weeks to keep a constant supply of flowers for cutting.

Schizanthus **

Also called the poor man's orchid, Schizanthus is very free-flowering and gives massed color in the spring garden. It is best in semi-shade, although it can be grown in the sun in temperate gardens. Schizanthus makes a wonderful display plant for hanging baskets or pots in filtered sun (a great greenhouse plant for cold areas). Seed can be sown from late summer to autumn (and early winter in warmer areas). Pots of advanced bedding plants are available from nurseries for quick and easy results. This is a free-flowering and disease-free plant with sprays of small, orchid-like flowers in white, pinks, crimson to violet shades all with markings in gold and contrasting colors.

Tip: If growing in hanging baskets, use a special potting mix for hanging baskets to help keep these plants from drying out between waterings.

Snapdragon **

Snapdragon seed can be sown throughout the year in most areas. Sow in autumn for spring flowers, spring for summer blooms. Sow in seedling boxes or pots or save time by buying advanced plants. There are tall and short varieties and many modern snapdragons have lost their "snap" and have large, ruffled flowers. All need good drainage, good air circulation and at least six hours of full sun a day. Tall varieties are great for a garden display and cut flowers. Dwarf varieties suit borders and containers on sunny balconies and patios. Prepare soil with organic matter and a dressing of complete fertilizer plus a light dressing of lime if soil is acid. Space tall varieties 16 inches (40cm) apart, dwarf 10 inches (25cm). Give liquid fertilizer when buds start.

Tip: Snapdragons are susceptible to rust—if this is a problem, grow varieties that are rust resistant, such as camelot and tetra mixed.

Statice ***

A good choice for warm and seaside gardens, statice is one of the "everlastings" which can be dried easily. Colors range from white and lemon to pink, mauve, and blue shades. It must have full sun and excellent drainage and stands dry, sandy soils. Though germination is erratic and may take up to 28 days, it is easy to grow from seed (from autumn to spring in warm to temperate areas). Sow in clumps where it is to grow and thin to strongest plants when seedlings develop true leaves. Bedding plants may be available. Prepare soil before planting with some compost and complete fertilizer and give side dressings when plants are half grown.

Tip: Statice is a perennial, though often grown as an annual, and if cut back will re-flower next season. To dry, cut and hang upside down in loose bunches in a cool, dry, airy place.

Stock **

Stock is wonderful for fragrant late-winter and spring flowers, which are good for cutting as well as garden display. Plants are double or single in mauve, purple, wine, pink, cream, lemon, and white. In suitable climates (those with dry summers and cool, wet winters) they will re-seed freely. Sow seed from mid-summer (autumn in warmer districts) or buy advanced bedding plants from mid-August. Plant out in a full sun position into soil with good drainage that has been prepared with compost or manure plus a handful of complete fertilizer forked into the top 6–8 inches (15–20cm) of soil. Stock seed germinates readily and can be sown direct or raised in seedling boxes. Plants should be spaced about 8 inches (20cm) apart for dwarf varieties but allow 12–16 inches (30–40cm) for tall ones such as giant perfection.

Tip: In heavy soils, raise beds 6 inches (15cm) to improve drainage—stocks won't tolerate wet feet.

Swan River Daisy **

The Swan River daisy, *Brachycome iberidifolia*, is a delightful, free-flowering native daisy growing to 8 inches (20cm) and forming neat clumps in baskets and other containers, borders, and rockeries. Colors are white, blue, pink, and mauve and there are now named varieties. Sow seed in spring either in seedling boxes or direct. The five-minute gardener, especially balcony gardeners, can save time by buying small plants already in bloom.

Tip: Plants flower year-round in warm and temperate climates. An occasional clip after blooming will encourage a fresh flush of flowers and keep plants neat.

Sweet Pea **

Sweet pea is a must for the picking garden and is one of the most fragrant of annuals. Tall varieties must have a trellis (running north-south), tripod or similar frame for climbing in full sun. Dwarf plants don't need support but form a bushy mound from 10–24 inches (25–60cm) high and suit rockeries, borders, window boxes and other containers on sunny balconies. Drainage must be good and beds in heavy soil should be raised up by 8 inches (20cm). Sweet peas like alkaline soil and in average garden soils 1½ tablespoons per square foot (1 cup per square meter) of lime or dolomite can be added (double this for heavy clay soils). Before planting, add a good layer of compost or manure and one third of a cup of complete fertilizer to the soil. Fork through the top 5 inches (12cm) of the soil, then loosen soil to spade depth, keeping the prepared layer on the surface. Water and leave for a week then rake over to scuff up any weeds and prepare soil for sowing. Water bed the night before planting so that soil is damp-dark. Press seeds down 1 inch (2–3cm) at 17 feet (5m) intervals. If soil is heavy, cover with vermiculite. Do not water until plants appear unless soil is very dry. When plants are 6 inches (15cm) help them attach to the wire with some small twigs.

Tip: Dust seed with fungicide before planting. Seed can be pre-germinated by spreading on wet toweling or mixed with moist vermiculite. Plant as soon as seeds swell. Don't discard small, shriveled seeds—these are darker colors.

Torenia *

This native of Vietnam is a great choice for the five-minute gardener. It stands up to summer heat and storms and flowers for months, right through autumn. It grows in full sun but will tolerate some filtered shade. Torenia is usually seen in two shades of blue with a yellow throat, but new varieties are pink, white, and mauve. Seed can be sown in spring and early summer, direct in clumps or in seedling boxes. It can also be bought in pots as advanced seedlings in mini-pots in bloom. Prepare soil with a tablespoon of complete fertilizer per square foot (a handful per square meter). Torenia suits borders, rockeries, and containers. Water in dry weather and give liquid fertilizer when buds form.

Tip: Plant for an autumn display with marigolds or yellow and white zinnia little star.

Verbena **

Verbena is a trailing plant that can be grown as a perennial in climates that aren't too hot and humid. This plant needs good drainage and full sun where it will flower for months through the warm weather. Plants grow to 12 inches (30cm) and colors include a range of pastels, many with a white eye. Seed is slow to germinate so pots of advanced bedding plants are the best choice for the five-minute gardener.

Tip: Verbena looks sensational grown over a sunny rock garden or brick edging. It enjoys the warmth of the bricks or rocks and revels in the quick drainage.

Vinca *

A popular new addition to annual displays, vinca (periwinkle) is really a perennial and, cut back after flowering, will re-grow and flower the following year in frost-free climates, flowering freely for months through the hottest weather. New varieties are pink, white, and cyclamen, and many have a contrasting eye.

Tip: Vinca is a fabulous color maker in seaside, subtropical and tropical gardens.

Virginia Stock *

Virginia stock is an easily grown little annual (to 8 inches/20cm) that can be sown where it is to grow in autumn or spring. Flowers are a mix of white, lilac, and pink shades and plants flower rapidly from seed. Will grow in any soil in full sun and will tolerate some shade. Encourage with liquid fertilizer when buds form.

Tip: Use as a cover plant over plantings of bulbs to keep down weeds and give a blanket of color.

Wallflower **

This wonderfully fragrant cottage garden plant has a shrubby habit to 24 inches (60 cm). Plant it in a sunny position sheltered from strong winds in well-drained soil prepared with compost or rotted manures plus a dressing of complete fertilizer forked through the soil. If soil is acid, add a dressing of lime (1½ tablespoons per square foot/1 cup per square meter). Sow seed in seedling boxes of seed raising mix from mid-summer to autumn for winter and early-spring flowers or look for advanced bedding plants from mid-August. Plant out 8 inches (20cm) apart in clumps. Give liquid fertilizer every two weeks when buds form. Wallflowers make good cut flowers.

Tip: Wallflowers belong to the cabbage family so watch for similar pests and diseases including cabbage butterfly caterpillar. Winter delight is recommended for cutting.

Zinnia **

Zinnia is a reliable summer-flowering annual that gives a long-flowering display and plenty of good cut flowers—a must for the picking garden. There are dwarf, medium, and tall varieties as well as the rockery zinnia little star. Sow seed in spring in seedling boxes or buy pots in late spring or early summer. Zinnias need full sun and well-drained soil. Improve soil before planting with added compost or manure plus a complete fertilizer. Plants should be about 16 inches (40cm) apart for tall growers and 8 inches (20cm) for dwarf varieties. This plant is ideal for hot, dry summers and in humid areas mildew may be a problem in late-summer (spray with fungicide).

Tip: Use dwarf varieties such as Thumbelina, little star, and Persian carpet in troughs or window boxes on sunny balconies.